CLEAN and LEAN FOR LIFE
The Cookbook

James Duigan

with Maria Lally

James Duigan, world-renowned wellness guru and owner of
Bodyism, London's premier health and wellness facility, is one
of the world's top personal trainers. Bodyism's glittering client
list has included Elle Macpherson, Lara Stone, Rosie Huntington-Whiteley,
David Gandy, Holly Valance and Hugh Grant. He is also the
author of the bestselling *Clean & Lean Diet*, *Clean & Lean Flat Tummy Fast!*,
Clean & Lean Diet Cookbook and *Clean & Lean Warrior*.

CLEAN *and* LEAN FOR LIFE
The Cookbook

150 DELICIOUS RECIPES FOR A HAPPY, HEALTHY BODY

James Duigan

with Maria Lally

Photography by Kate Davis-Macleod and Clare Winfield
Shot on location at the D-Hotel Maris, Turkey

KYLE BOOKS

This edition published in 2015 by
Kyle Books, an imprint of Kyle Cathie Ltd
192–198 Vauxhall Bridge Road
London, SW1V 1DX
general.enquiries@kylebooks.com
www.kylebooks.com

10 9 8 7 6 5 4 3 2 1

ISBN 978 0 85783 334 1

Editor: Judith Hannam
Assistant editor: Vicki Murrell
Editorial assistant: Hannah Coughlin
Design: Dale Walker
Models: Christiane Duigan
Location styling: D-Hotel Maris, Turkey
Food stylist: Emily Kydd
Prop stylist: Iris Bromet
Copy editor: Caroline McArthur and Daniella Isaacs
Recipe contributors: Daniella Isaacs and
Rebecca Sullivan
Production: Lisa Pinnell

A Cataloguing in Publication record for this title
is available from the British Library.

Colour reproduction by ALTA London
Printed and bound in China by C&C Offset
Printing Co., Ltd.

The information and advice contained in this book
are intended as a general guide. Neither the author
nor the publishers can be held responsible for claims
arising from the inappropriate use of any remedy
or exercise regime. Do not attempt self-diagnosis
or self-treatment for serious or long-term conditions
before consulting a medical professional or qualified
practitioner. Do not begin any exercise programme
or undertake any self-treatment while taking other
prescribed drugs or receiving therapy without
first seeking professional guidance. Always seek
medical advice if any symptoms persist.

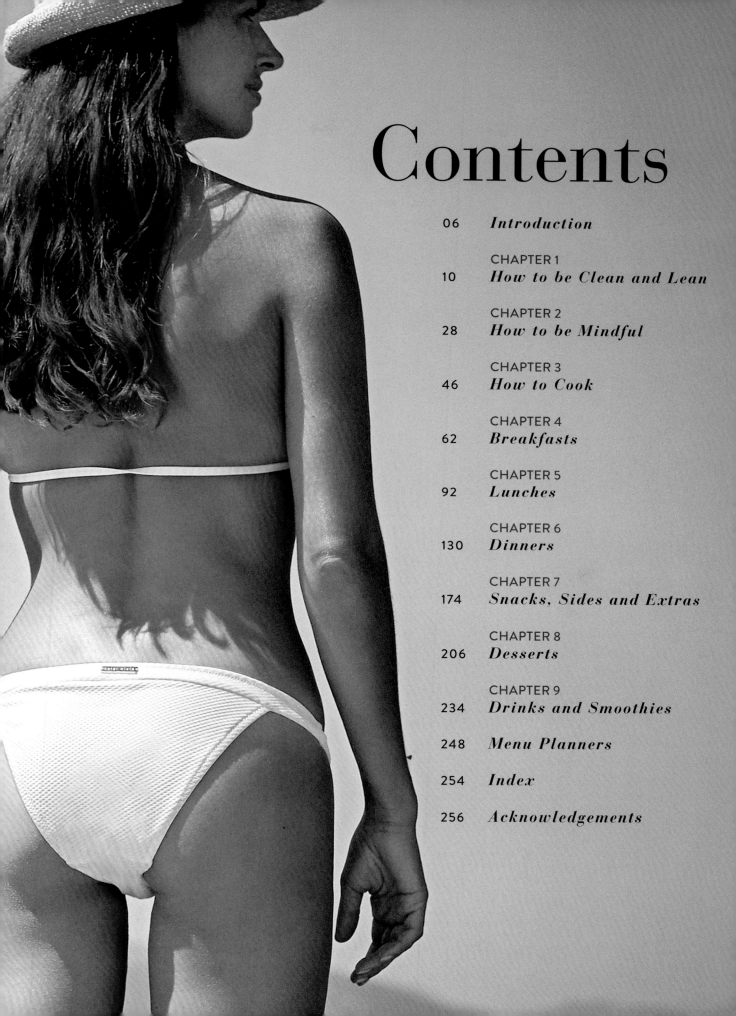

Contents

Introduction

This beautiful book is full of delicious foods and simple recipes that are wonderfully Clean and Lean. Yes, they will help you lose weight but, more importantly, they will help you feel good. Every ingredient and combination of foods has been chosen with your health in mind, so relax and enjoy the ride.

This book has also been written with busy people in mind, so the recipes are simple and easy to prepare, with ingredients that you can get just about anywhere. This book is not about challenging your cooking skills. It is about helping you to become a healthier, happier, more energised version of your self. There are a few points to remember that will really help you on your health journey. Firstly, diets don't work – they just don't. Making profound and lasting changes is not possible when you do something for just a couple of weeks. In fact, most diets will result in weight gain as well as often making you sick and miserable. If something sounds crazy, then it probably is. Please don't ruin your health, and I mean both your physical health and your mental health. The key to success is keeping it simple. If you are weighing your food or your poo (yes, some people do this), counting calories, only eating cabbage or only drinking chinese herbs (yes, these are things), then you are doing it all wrong and it won't work. In order to transform your body, you need to change your life in a way that is enjoyable and sustainable, and the good news is it's really very easy.

Remember that any change in your body happens in your mind first. This is where you need to really understand that you deserve to be healthy and happy and once you do this, all the choices you have been struggling with will suddenly become easy and effortless. You will no longer sabotage yourself with crazy fad diets or mountains of junk food because you will know that you deserve perfect health and a perfect body. 'A perfect body', you ask? What is the perfect body? It is the body that you are healthy and happy in. You may be happy being very underweight or very overweight, but you're not healthy and that is just a medical and biological reality. You may also have a really healthy body and yet you're constantly miserable because you're never happy with how you look, which is all too common and too sad for words. So you need both. You need to be happy and healthy, and that my friends is the perfect body. And it really is possible, regardless of what you may have believed in the past. Your past does not equal your future and right now, in this very moment, you have an incredible opportunity to finally succeed in making a permanent and beautiful transformation. Self acceptance is the key here and letting go of shame and guilt is essential. No more beating yourself up, no more pointing out the negative. Let go of the past, stop seeing it as a series of failures and see them as they actually are – a series of powerful lessons for you to learn from. Now is the time to empower yourself with kind and positive thoughts, words and actions. You are beautiful and powerful and you never need to doubt that. Now all you have to do is trust yourself and start living a...

Clean and Lean life!

A way of life

I also want to share a little story about myself in the hope that it may help you understand that we are all just doing our best and that we are all human and vulnerable to what life puts in our path. My beautiful dad was my best friend and my hero and in 2012 he was diagnosed with stage 4 lung cancer. We completely changed his diet by cutting out all sugar, dairy and red meat, we got him doing yoga, visualisations, drinking vegetable juices with turmeric and whatever else we could think of, and when Dad went in for his next appointment 3 months later, his cancer had completely disappeared. We were all so grateful and happy and cherished every moment we had with each other as a family. We had two more beautiful years with him and then the cancer came back very aggressively. I went back to Australia to help him fight for his life. I remember him saying that he knew he would beat it because I was there with him... but I couldn't do it. My dad believed in me and I failed him. I couldn't save him, and telling my mother and my sister that Dad had just passed away was the hardest thing I have ever done. As I walked into the house I was ashamed that I hadn't been able to save him. I felt so sad for my family and I felt very alone. So how did I cope with this? I comforted myself with food. I had been eating potatoes and rice and pasta with dad (he needed to keep his weight up) so he didn't feel lonely... and I just didn't stop. My weight really went up and I put on ten kilos very quickly. I wasn't comfortable or happy but I didn't care. It all seemed so trivial next to losing dad but as I came out of the haze of the first stages of grief I noticed that I really didn't feel healthy at all. I decided to become more mindful about what I was eating, which helped a little, but nothing really happened and I still felt like I had let everyone down. I spend my life telling people to let go of shame and guilt and here I was, carrying it around everywhere I went like a dark cloud. It was Chrissy who very gently pointed out to me that it was time to forgive myself, that it wasn't my fault and I could not have done any more to save my dad... and I knew she was right, but I just couldn't quite let go of it. I was almost comfortable with my shame and guilt and I felt like my grief was my only way of holding on to my dad. However, I also knew I had to do something different, so I really worked on it, every day. Sometimes, every minute, and eventually I was able to let my shame and guilt go and I began to feel good about myself again, and when this happened I began to choose more kindly for myself. I was eating better and enjoying life and as a consequence, almost effortlessly I lost ten kilos in 3 months. I've learnt to smile again and now the memories of my father mostly bring a smile rather than tears. So whatever you're going through, no matter how many times you feel you've failed, just know that you're not alone and that right now is the time to forgive yourself and begin living the life of your dreams.

> Whatever you're going through, no matter how many times you feel you've failed, just know that you're not alone.

As I was writing this introduction, I read a study that states '40% of girls between the age of 3 and 5 are worried they are fat'... as if I haven't cried enough writing this thing. I looked at my amazing, kind, talented and intelligent daughter and I just wanted to pick her up and protect her from all of this forever. But I can't do that, so I'm going to change the world instead. If you are lucky enough to have children, please don't ever focus on their weight or how they look. It. Will. Mess. Them. Up. I hear stories of parents who weigh their children every day at breakfast and after dinner – it's heartbreaking. It is why we have girls (and boys) on social media hijacking genuinely good messages about being 'strong not skinny' next to a picture of an anorexic body in a bikini promoting a 'bikini body guide' or posting about being 'strong empowered women' and 'by the way here's a picture of my butt in a G-string or knickers' (I tried this and lost a lot of followers, but that's a different story!). My point is, please be mindful of the words you use around your children and the people you love. And don't take your health, exercise and nutritional advice from a 23-year-old on social media who has done a 6-week personal training course and has absolutely zero accountability for anything they say. You deserve better and so do our children.

chapter 1

HOW TO BE
CLEAN
AND
LEAN

It's been six years since I wrote the first Clean and Lean book and to say a lot has changed in health and wellness since then would be an understatement. Back then I battled with my publishers to include ingredients like kale and quinoa because nobody had ever heard of them. Now they're available in every supermarket. In fact they're cooler than any vegetable in history because they even have their own t-shirts. When I told readers to cook with coconut oil instead of olive oil, hundreds wrote to me asking where to buy it or what to do with it. Now it's written about, available and used everywhere. People are also putting it on their hair, skin and in their coffee. Back then, Facebook was full of holiday and baby photos, now – along with every other form of social media including Twitter and Instagram – it's full of people showing pictures of their morning green juice, superfood salad or workout session with their own customised playlists. Health, it would seem, has never been hotter.

But one thing hasn't changed – at all – and that's my advice. Diet fads and exercise trends have come and gone in the last six years. But everything I said then, I stand by today. And better still, leading scientists around the world have since confirmed that what we said back then is true.

Clean and Lean is a long-term lifestyle with incredible results – it's a journey of empowerment where every step is healthier and more beautiful. There are no dogmatic rules to follow or break. It's not just another way to fail, like a lot diets, instead it's a blueprint for success.

Six years ago I devoted a whole chapter to sugar, and why it is a dangerous substance that makes us fat, sick, tired and prematurely wrinkled. When I wrote about it in 2009 there wasn't a lot of awareness about the dangers of sugar. Sure, people knew it rotted your teeth and too many sweets weren't good you, but back then people had no idea how dangerous over-consumption of sugar was for almost every aspect of your health – for your heart, your liver, your risk of developing diabetes or cancer. We were paying very little attention to all the added sugars lurking in our food, which were making us fat and ill, focusing instead on calories and fat.

But gradually the anti-sugar message got out. Several major health studies about sugar were written and in 2015 the World Health Organisation – the specialised

'SUGAR IS ONE OF THE BIGGEST HEALTH ISSUES OF OUR GENERATION'

agency of the United Nations (UN) concerned with public health – issued a statement warning everybody to dramatically cut their sugar intake. They advised reducing it to 10% of our daily calorie intake. And this was just a bare minimum requirement – they suggested a further reduction to 5% to see any health benefits. I think this will drop even further in the future once more studies back up my firmly held belief that sugar is one of the biggest health issues of our generation.

I devoted another chapter of the book to fat. Back then people were very fat phobic and this meant whole natural foods – like butter, red meat and even eggs – were out and low-fat processed foods full of sugar were in. And what a disaster that has proved to be.

I knew from my studies, and from years of meeting clients who were gaining weight on low-fat diets full of processed sugar, that this approach didn't work. I could see we'd grown fat on the low-fat message. We need to embrace (clean) fat because it keeps us full, makes our hair shine, gives us energy, boosts our concentration levels and makes our food taste so great that we don't need to overeat or look for sugar after a meal. When I talk about 'clean' fat, I'm talking about natural, unprocessed fat. Not some funky junk from a packet, processed cheap meat, donuts or biscuits, but succulent (organic, if possible) free-range meats, avocado, nuts, seeds, oils and butter (keep it 'clean' by buying the organic kind, ideally from grass-fed cows).

And just like cutting down on sugar, my advice to embrace fat has been proven correct. In the last few years scientists have admitted official guidelines about fat have been way off the mark and that, rather than fat, we should in fact be worrying about processed carbohydrates and sugar. As I write this book in May 2015, the US government is planning to drop cholesterol from its list of 'nutrients of concern' and is set to focus on sugar instead.

So, in short, Clean and Lean isn't a fad, it's a powerful way to change your life. It's also been proven to work. It's a way of eating, moving and living that you can trust to make you feel healthier and happier. In this book I'm going to teach you how to be mindful, and how to cook Clean and Lean. I've shared 150 wonderful recipes so that you can stay Clean and Lean for life. But before I do that, here's a quick reminder of what it means to be Clean and Lean.

CLEAN AND LEAN WORKS

What is CLEAN and LEAN?

For those of you new to the Clean and Lean concept, it is a term I use to describe how our body wants to be. Its natural state is to be clean of toxins (found in processed foods and in the environment around us) and lean (slim, strong and energised – but not skinny).

First let me quickly explain what I mean when I talk about 'toxins' as there has been some debate around the use of this word in relation to our health. Some people have taken offence to the term being used incorrectly – so let me apologise in advance to anyone who feels this way. For the purposes of this book, a toxin refers to any substance that is harming you and your health. Is sugar a harmful toxin in tiny doses? Nope, but most of the world is consuming it in harmful, and therefore toxic, quantities. For this reason it's an appropriate term to use here. If anyone doubts this I would refer them to obesity and diabetes statistics and then ask them if they are still happy to play semantics and sound thrillingly intelligent. I wrote this book to help, not to sound clever. I wrote it to change people's lives. Anyway, on with the book.

Your body wants to be lean, strong, nourished and healthy. It doesn't feel happy or strong being starved, deprived or exercised to exhaustion. But it also doesn't feel happy carrying lots of excess fat. I'm not skinny- or fat-shaming anybody with these words, I'm just stating medical fact. Our bodies are healthiest when they're somewhere between these two extremes – when they're strong and slim.

Of course, everybody has a different body shape – some of us are naturally tall and lean, some tall and broad. Others are athletically built, while some are short and petite, or curvaceous. Many are somewhere in between, or a bit of a mix. There's no 'right' body shape and some of us are naturally predisposed to carry more fat or muscle in certain areas than others. But regardless of body shape, everybody can be slim, healthy and happy.

The diet and food industries will tell you this is hard. Your friends and family may tell you it's hard. You may even tell yourself it's hard, shamed by memories of failed diets and weight struggles. But it's really not hard if you know the right way to do it. It's this simple – eat Clean and Lean, move your body everyday and be mindful. If you do these things your body will find its natural, happy weight very easily.

So remember – your body wants to be lean and you deserve to be happy and healthy. Our bodies are designed to be lean and healthy and it's very easy to get them this way. But our modern lifestyle – full of 'convenience' food (ironic, because there's nothing convenient about feeling uncomfortably full and overweight), alcohol, too much coffee, too much stress and too little movement – is stopping that from happening.

Toxins found in processed foods affect the way our bodies hold on to fat, resulting in squidgy bits of excess flesh around our stomachs, waists, thighs, hips, faces and arms. We feel bloated and tired and look older than we should. Ironically, feeling this way makes us crave more processed, toxic food and the depressing cycle continues. We get fatter, feel worse and crave more bad food that makes us fatter still. We need to break this cycle and we can do this by becoming Clean and Lean.

Clean and Lean isn't about calorie counting, cutting food groups or worrying about the scientific makeup of certain foods. So read on, follow each easy step and discover how good it feels (and how easy it is) to have the body you deserve.

Why do TOXINS MAKE US FAT?

When I talk about 'Clean' I mean clean from toxins. Your body will never be lean unless it's Clean. Toxins stop your body from being Clean because your body stores toxins in its fat cells. If you're dieting but your body is full of toxins, it may lose fat but the toxins will have nowhere to go but back into your system. You'll feel tired, lethargic and you may have headaches, which is why many of us feel terrible when we're on a diet. Your body decides it doesn't like feeling this way so it holds on to fat in order to have somewhere to store the toxins. If you have a high toxic load you'll always struggle to lose weight. And, ironically, many diets make us more toxic with their low fat/high sugar and chemical advice, so the cycle of yo-yo dieting continues.

Oh, and a word on chemicals. Again some people have pointed out that everything we eat is made up of 'chemicals'. Yes, they are correct, but they are missing the point and people's lives are at stake. When we talk about chemicals in the food we eat we aren't talking about 'the basic building blocks of all matter', we are talking about the nasty chemical additives that are added to so many foods found on supermarket shelves and in pre-packaged, processed foods. Remember, if in doubt eat fruit, vegetables and free-range meat or fish, and make it organic if you can.

SO WHERE ARE TOXINS MOSTLY FOUND?

* Sugar
* Alcohol
* Processed food (including 'diet' foods)
* Excess caffeine

SUGAR

Ditching sugar is possibly the most important principle of the Clean and Lean diet. It makes you look older and feel fat, tired and sick and it's one of the first things I tell a client to remove from their diet. Here's why.

1 It makes you fat

The pancreas controls the level of sugar in our blood. If the pancreas is overloaded and can't process excess sugar efficiently, that sugar gets stored as fat. Sugar also stops your body burning fat and it makes you crave more sugar (see below). Put simply – if you're eating a lot of sugar every day (and remember, it's found in pasta sauces, cereal and yogurt, as well as the more obvious things like chocolate and sweets), you will always find it difficult (did someone say impossible?) to lose weight. And being overweight increases your risk of other illnesses, including certain cancers, heart disease and diabetes. Plus, if you're very overweight it reduces your quality of life. This is serious.

2 It's addictive

In fact, it's one of the most addictive substances in our lives. Sugar makes you crave sugar because it gives you an opium-like high. When you stop eating sugar for a while something amazing happens – you stop craving it. Eventually you lose the taste for it altogether and by the time this happens you'll feel slimmer, healthier and your skin will look younger and smoother. Please be kind to yourself and let this addiction to sugar go. Try it – I promise it works.

3 It depletes vitamin and mineral stores in the body

This weakens your immune system and leaves you emotionally and physically worn out.

4 It converts to fat quicker than fat

Burning body fat is all about controlling your insulin levels. Sugar spikes raise your insulin levels leading to fat storage and this is the real reason why so many of us in the Western world are either overweight or obese. Sugar is making us fatter and that fat goes straight to our hips, stomach and thighs. Every time you eat too much sugar you're adding to that fat. Ditch the sugar and you'll drop the fat so much easier.

5 It makes you tired

Excess sugar quickly increases your blood sugar levels, giving you a buzz (that 'sugar high' many of us chase in the afternoons when we're feeling tired). But this quick burst of energy is fleeting and is soon replaced by a hard crash that leaves you even more tired than you were before. And – yep, you guessed it – craving more sugar. Stop the sugar cycle!

6 It wears out your organs

Sugar makes your kidneys and pancreas work too hard as they try to deal with this awful foreign substance that shouldn't be there. It effectively makes your pancreas age very quickly, which will eventually lead it to fail, which is essentially what diabetes is.

Where is SUGAR USUALLY FOUND?

White refined sugar

The type you stir into your tea.

Fruit juices

Most are just sugared water with very little, or none, of the fibre, vitamin and mineral content left. The occasional glass won't do much harm, but it won't do you much good either. If you drink fruit juice or squash all day you're simply drip-feeding sugar into your body.

White carbohydrates

White, non-organic pasta, bread and rice, cereals and cereal bars are all high in sugar. Opt for different types of grains like quinoa or teff, and don't fall into the bread and pasta every day trap.

Alcohol

It's the simplest sugar of all and is, in my opinion, like a nuclear fat bomb on your body, especially wine and beer. Like fruit juice, the odd glass won't hurt, but don't drink it every day or to excess.

Low-fat foods

Foods like yogurts, most breakfast cereals, cereal bars, salad dressings, yogurt-covered raisins, muffins and other foods labelled 'low-fat' or 'no-fat' are nearly always stuffed with sugar. Read the label and avoid them... like really avoid them – back away slowly and don't make eye contact.

Ingredients ending in '-ose' or '-oxe'

It's simply sugar hiding behind another name, such as sucrose, glucose, maltose, lactose, dextrose and fructose. 'Syrup' is also basically sugar, as is 'high-fructose corn syrup', which is just about the worst type of sugar you can eat. Many food manufacturers and shops have stopped using it altogether, but it's still around. It's one of the cheapest and nastiest sweeteners and boosts fat-storing hormones as well as increasing your risk of certain diseases and reducing your fertility.

HOW TO GIVE IT UP

Have protein and a little fat with every meal

Sugar cravings often come from a lack of both. Darker meats in particular – like beef and lamb, chicken thighs, liver etc. – contain more purines, which make them more filling and therefore reduce sugar cravings.

Take a glutamine supplement

This is an amino acid that's available in most health stores and reduces sugar cravings as well as helping general gut health.

Don't use sugar as a reward

It's not a reward – it's a horrible, unhealthy toxin that will make you fat and increase your chances of getting sick. It will break down the collagen in your skin and give you premature lines and wrinkles. It will make you constantly hungry and it will make you feel tired every day. How is that a treat? Sugar is not your friend. Sugar is a bitch who is trying to ruin your life and steal your boyfriend.

Include chromium in your diet

It helps control your blood sugar levels, which helps to reduce sugar cravings. Chromium can be found in eggs, nuts, mushrooms and asparagus.

ALCOHOL

Alcohol is basically a very sugary poison. Just like with sugar, you'll never be as lean as you could be if you drink alcohol every day, or most days. Terms like 'beer belly' and 'wine waist' are used for a reason – alcohol simply creates a ring of fat right around our mid sections.

As well as being full of sugar, alcohol contains phytoestrogen, which promotes fat storage and decreases muscle growth. So if you go to the gym but also drink regularly, all that lovely lean muscle you've created via exercise to keep you looking toned, will turn squidgy.

The liver is also a fat-burning organ – and when it's busy trying to process all those glasses of wine, it's not doing its proper job. For every drink you have you're slowing your metabolism right down and you're encouraging fat storage. So you're getting a double whammy of fat gain. Now factor in the starchy, carb-heavy, salty or sweet foods you crave when you're hungover and you'll see why alcohol is a fat bomb that explodes all over your body. As well as the weight gain, prolonged and frequent

drinking also causes many health problems including liver conditions, a higher risk of several cancers, high blood pressure and a greater risk of heart attacks and reduced fertility. The scary thing about regular drinking is that the problems can often stay hidden for a long time and then emerge after many years. Which means you might be drinking a lot in your 20s and 30s, feeling confident it's not doing you much harm, but by your 40s or 50s real health problems will begin to emerge.

'ALCOHOL IS BASICALLY A SUGARY POISON'

I don't drink at all, but most of my clients drink occasionally so I'm realistic about alcohol. I train businessmen and women who drink wine a couple of times a week when eating out, or who like a glass of wine on a Friday night with dinner or a couple of beers with their Sunday roast. And generally this is fine. If you're otherwise healthy then this type of drinking – while not healthy – won't do you a huge amount of harm. But don't drink every day, or every other day, or so heavily you do stupid things or forget stuff. That's not healthy and will eventually damage your health.

'DON'T HAVE "CALORIE BLINDNESS" WITH YOUR DRINKS'

Excess CAFFEINE

I say 'excess' because caffeine isn't that bad – certainly nowhere near as bad as sugar, alcohol and processed food. In fact, it has a few health benefits and, if you enjoy it, caffeine can form a healthy part of your diet.

Most people have their caffeine in the form of coffee or tea, but it's worth remembering that it's also found in green tea, certain painkillers and cold and flu remedies, and chocolate.

I'm a coffee fan and a couple of cups of tea or coffee a day are fine. Caffeine isn't the problem, but the way we tend to drink it is. Huge lattes full of cows' milk and sugar, or worse those creamy flavoured frappuccinos, are loaded with processed junk and sugar. Many people have 'calorie blindness' with their drinks, but especially with their coffees. They 'forget' that their huge latte with sugar contains 200–300 calories, so they happily drink three of them. I'm not a fan of calorie counting, but calories (especially those from sugary sources) do add up, so keep an eye on what you're drinking. The key to coffee is to keep it Clean and Lean – in other words, keep it simple. Have it black and organic or with a little full-fat organic milk or cream. Organic coffee is packed with antioxidants and is great for digestion. It can also help your performance in the gym if you have it 30 minutes before exercise – studies show you can work out for longer if you have caffeine just before a workout. And sprinkle a little cinnamon in it to keep your blood sugar levels steady.

But you must stick to one or two cups of coffee, three cups of tea or four cups of green tea per day, and always try to have them before lunch.

Too much caffeine overstimulates your nervous system, causing you to pump out the stress hormone cortisol, which causes fat storage. So, if you drink coffee all day you're flooding your body with fat-storing hormones (generally around the front of the tummy). Too much caffeine also often means you're not drinking enough water, which is vital for flushing out your system and transporting all the goodness from your food around your body. Too much caffeine also disrupts sleep, and not enough sleep switches on your fat-storing hormones.

TOO MUCH CAFFEINE OVERSTIMULATES YOUR NERVOUS SYSTEM, CAUSING YOU TO PUMP OUT THE STRESS HORMONE CORTISOL, WHICH CAUSES FAT STORAGE.

Top tip!
*If you can't
pronounce the
ingredient's name,
don't eat it!*

Processed FOODS

*These go against every Clean and Lean rule there is.
As I've said before, the less a food has been altered, the
'Cleaner' it is. Processed foods are the very opposite of
this – they've been made in factories, stripped of their
natural goodness, altered, processed, pumped full of
toxic sweeteners, salt or preservatives and sometimes
dyed to look slightly less disgusting.*

THE WORST PROCESSED FOODS

* Breakfast cereals
* Chocolate, sweets and crisps
* Frozen chips, wedges etc.
* Frozen meat or fish that's breaded or battered
* Packaged cakes, biscuits, muffins
* Processed meats
* Ready meals
* Tinned foods
* White bread, pasta and rice

Why aren't processed foods 'Clean'?

One method of preserving processed food is to hyper heat it, which means most of the health-boosting vitamins, fibre and minerals it naturally contains are lost. This is why fresh fruit is better for us than tinned fruit that has been heated and stored for months. Do you really think all that lovely vitamin C found in a fresh peach will survive this process?

Vitamins and minerals don't just keep us healthy and ward off disease and illness, they also keep us full and nourished. A body that's well nourished will feel satisfied. A malnourished person – one who is living on ready meals and processed food – will feel hungry all the time because they're not getting any nutrients. Just so you know, there are millions of very overweight people who are, ironically and tragically, malnourished.

As well as reducing the nutritional value of food, processing has other implications for our health. Our bodies can't cope – and weren't designed to cope – with all the artificial flavourings, colourings, preservatives and other additives that are frequently added to processed foods to make them look and taste better, and last longer. Avoid them by sticking to Clean, simple and delicious foods.

What are CLEAN FOODS?

1 They haven't changed a great deal from their natural state

For example, an apple in a bowl looks like an apple on a tree. But bread, crisps and pasta don't look like they did in the beginning. That's because they've been processed to become a type of food. In a nutshell, Clean foods haven't been tampered with. They may have been altered slightly, but generally they look, taste and smell like they did in the beginning.

2 They don't have any added fake flavour

They're not covered in a dusting of artificial salty flavour or sweetened with a sickly sugar coating. Their natural flavour is all that's needed to make them taste great. Juicy prawns, succulent steak, creamy egg, tender green vegetables that are in season and sweet, fresh berries are delicious just as they are. They don't need added flavours because they're Clean whole foods.

3 They don't last for months in your cupboard or fridge

I've heard of bright red, shiny tomatoes that stay fresh in the fridge for weeks and weeks. That's not normal. Clean foods go off. They develop mould, droop, wilt and go brown. They're natural, Clean and unprocessed. They don't contain fake and toxic additives and preservatives to keep them fresh for weeks on end. That's not right and it's definitely not Clean.

4 They don't have a huge list of ingredients, many of which you can't even pronounce

In fact, truly Clean foods only have one ingredient that they don't even need to list. Kale, asparagus, chicken, eggs, coconut oil, prawns – they come as they are. Other Clean foods may contain ingredients, but only a few. For example, natural yoghurt, cheese, oatcakes or rye bread.

5 Sugar isn't one of the first ingredients

Or in fact any part of the ingredients list. Food packaging lists ingredients proportionally – so whatever they contain most of is mentioned first. If the word sugar – or words meaning sugar (see page 19) – are lurking anywhere near the top of the ingredients list, put it down and choose something simpler and Cleaner instead.

6 They don't make you feel bloated or uncomfortable after eating

They don't make you windy or burp a lot. Your body – especially your tummy – is the best guide you have as to whether a food is Clean and good for you. If it makes you gassy then it's probably not Clean.

7 They satisfy you

When you eat a lovely Clean salad with protein and healthy fats like nuts or oil, you feel happily full and satisfied. Compare that to how you feel when you eat something toxic or processed. After a greasy takeaway burger you feel tired, full, gassy and then crave something sweet. After a bowl of pasta you might feel the same. After a ready meal – which contains hardly any filling protein or healthy fats – you feel hungry an hour later. Clean foods satisfy you, and as a side note, I'm pretty sure Mick Jagger was eating processed foods when he wrote the song '(I can't get no) Satisfaction'.

EAT FAT

As I said at the start of this chapter, don't be fat phobic. Good Clean fats should be eaten every day and with every meal. They encourage your body to burn fat around the middle and they also help you to absorb the vitamins and minerals from your food more efficiently. In fact, if you have a salad or vegetables always eat them with a little fat (like an avocado or some nuts) so that you absorb all their goodness. Fat also reduces sugar cravings, makes you more alert, and makes your skin, hair and nails look better.

What if you're a vegetarian?

Vegetarians can easily follow the Clean and Lean programme. Include lots of vegetarian proteins in your diet from legumes such as beans, lentils and chickpeas. Rather than rely too heavily on bread and pasta, eat grains such as quinoa, oats and wild rice. And have lots of good fats from walnuts, pecans, almonds, Brazil nuts, sesame, flax and pumpkin seeds.

HERE'S WHERE TO FIND GOOD FAT

* Avocados
* Coconut oil
* Extra virgin olive oil
* Nuts
* Oily fish
* Organic goats' butter
* Organic goats' cheese
* Seeds
* Unsalted organic butter from grass-fed cows

The downside to HEALTH AWARENESS

At the beginning of this chapter I talked about how these days we're all so much more aware of our health. As I said earlier, social media nowadays is just as likely to be filled with photos of your green juice as it is your holiday photos. And in many ways this is a brilliant thing. People are more aware of their health than ever. Wellness is the new status symbol and a green juice is the new It handbag. And surely more people being into their health can only be a good thing? Well, yes and no.

While I love the fact that health has never been more talked about, I worry a great deal about all the misinformation and insanity out there. Many people giving advice today – especially those online and on social media – are ruining people's lives with '12 week bikini guides' that promote anorexia and prescribe dangerous exercise programmes that injure bodies and destroy self esteem. The rise of the 'Instagram anorexic' is truly frightening and these ruthless self-promoters have no shame. They have hijacked wonderful messages of strength and confidence by posting constant images of themselves in bikinis or underwear looking, quite frankly, malnourished. While there are some amazing food and health bloggers out there, there are also plenty telling their, in some cases, millions of followers to restrict calories or do intense plyometric training, or both. So sad and so scary.

What is even more worrying is the complete lack of accountability. These people are handing out damaging advice with no consequences at all. Some are even sponsored by companies or are paid to post. What's more, at the time of writing, they don't have to state this on their websites! That's crazy. These people can say pretty much whatever they want – and make any claim – with zero accountability.

Wellness online is the new Wild West – it's pretty dangerous out there so be careful. Don't start eating nothing but bananas because someone in a bikini with a million followers on Instagram tells you to (yes, this is a real thing).

Keep things simple and remember that good health is accessible. You don't need to spend a fortune working out. The world is your gym and your body is the best piece of equipment you have. Your living room is a great place to get fit, as is your park. Or simply move around a lot more by walking everywhere and doing body weight exercises. Similarly with food, eating well doesn't cost a lot and it shouldn't be exclusive, expensive or tricky. So forget the gimmicks and keep things simple – eat well, move more and be mindful.

If you take nothing else from this book, take this – question everything. If it sounds crazy, it probably is. And running around in a bikini does not qualify you to advise people on how to eat or exercise. Please be careful and please be kind to yourself.

'DON'T TAKE HEALTH ADVICE FROM INSTAGRAM'

chapter 2

HOW TO BE
MINDFUL

Mindfulness has now become a health buzzword that's often talked about but not always fully understood. So what is mindfulness? It's really a very simple concept that involves finding some time and space in your day to be aware of what you're doing, tune in to your breathing, tune in to your body and really take note of how you are feeling. This might mean a couple of minutes out of a busy day to take a moment. Or to just slow down and really focus on what you're doing – like eating, working or being with someone you love. It's free, quick, you can do it anywhere and it allows you to feel calmer, happier and less stressed.

In the past I rushed through life trying to get everything done. I ate healthily but I worked, trained and lived to exhaustion. I rushed things and got stressed. I had a busy brain that whirred constantly and I did lots of things, but I flitted between them all and did them half-heartedly. I procrastinated and couldn't concentrate on one thing for very long. Becoming mindful wasn't something that happened for me overnight – it was more of a gradual process – but when it happened it was a wonderful revelation. My life was still just as busy, but I felt I had more time and space. I spent less time getting more done. Stressful things still happened in my life, but I didn't feel stressed by them (well, not as much as I did before). I felt happier – and that's why we're all here.

So how did I manage to become mindful? Well, I made a few simple changes, but also two things happened in my life that jolted me out of the 'mindlessly busy' rut I was in. One good, and one sad, but both beautiful in their own way. The first thing was the birth of my first child, Charlotte, in 2012. My wife Christiane and I had struggled to get pregnant, so when we finally conceived Charlotte, life changed forever. I enjoyed every single moment of Chrissy's pregnancy because I knew how hard we'd struggled to get there. Seeing Chrissy's beautiful tummy grow over the weeks and months was a very real and physical reminder of how time passes, which helped me appreciate how important every minute is. Every night I would talk and sing to her tummy. I felt connected to the world and completely content. When Charlotte was born something just clicked in my head

and I started living in the moment. For the first time in my life I was completely present. I didn't feel like I was missing out on anything because there was nowhere in the world I would rather be.

Then something sad happened. I lost my beautiful Dad to cancer and that too, was a wake-up call. I was fortunate enough to have the chance to tell my dad that I loved him at least a hundred times a day and I feel lucky that I could hug him every day and hear his voice. I am grateful that I was able to carry him when he was too weak to walk and blessed that I was there to feed him when he was too weak to feed himself. Because I knew that Dad was holding on with all his strength, but that it was a fight we might not win, I cherished every single minute, every single sound and smell and feeling in those moments. When my Dad finally died in my arms I knew that he felt completely loved and that he knew I loved him with all my heart. I know this because when I was there with him. I wasn't texting or Tweeting… I was there with him and nothing was more important than that. Because he was my hero and he deserved nothing less. So that was my lesson – that nothing is more important than being with the people you love. Really being with them, and for them to know that you love them with all your heart. That's just the best thing in the world.

'IN THE PAST I RUSHED THROUGH LIFE TRYING TO GET EVERYTHING DONE'

In the days after Dad passed away I thought I would be sad forever and that I would never smile again. But it passed and I found things to be grateful for in each beautiful moment of my life. It was being present in life that allowed me to move through my grief. For anyone who is having a tough time staying motivated, this story may help you get some perspective. My father's body had wasted away. He was very frail physically, but his spirit stayed strong. His last words were, 'I'm still fighting son, I haven't given up'. I know my dad was in pain during those last days, but he hid it from us all and he fought to stay alive to his last breath. Seeing his courage and strength inspired me to be stronger and kinder. I promised myself I would never give up, ever, no matter the odds. So if you're feeling like it's all too much, please remember that you are stronger than you'd ever imagine.

How to live
MINDFULLY

I now try to be very mindful every day, but I still slip up occasionally. When you're juggling work, family and home life, it's very easy to get sucked into that feeling of being too busy to breathe. Being mindful isn't something that happens and then just sticks – you have to maintain it, like having a garden or watering a plant. Here's how.

1 Be mindful of how you use technology

We have never been more addicted to our phones – and it's making us less mindful. It's also making us stressed, forgetful, anxious, and it's impacting on our overall health. Smartphone separation anxiety is actually a thing now. A 2014 study from Missouri University in the US found that when we don't have our smartphones close by, our heart rate, blood pressure and anxiety levels increase and our 'cognitive abilities' (in other words our intelligence and ability to think logically) decrease. Study participants performed puzzles better when they had their phones on them. When their phones were taken away or had little or no battery life they couldn't focus as well and performed worse at simple tasks.

The author of the study came up with the idea when he was having dinner with a friend who had forgotten their phone. The friend became anxious, couldn't concentrate on the conversation and wanted to leave to go and get it.

'YOUR PHONE IS NOT YOUR FRIEND, PUT IT DOWN AND BE WHERE YOU ARE'

This story really makes me sad. How have we come to a point where we'd rather spend time with a palm-sized electronic device than with our own friends and loved ones? I see it all the time – couples out to lunch who are ignoring each other because they're staring at their phones. There have been studies that have found some couples would rather browse on social media on their phones before bed than have sex. Then there are the parents at playgroup mindlessly scrolling on their phone instead of watching their children – who will never be that little again – having fun. Sure, some of them are probably checking important work emails, but there are probably some just catching up with what their friends – or acquaintances they haven't seen in years – are doing on Facebook. Don't be this person. The time and energy you invest in really connecting with your children and, in fact, everyone in your life, will pay off a thousand times over – your real, beautiful, magical life is happening all around you while you're on your phone.

I'm guilty of all this myself. I've often caught myself watching a TV show while browsing on my phone (in the past a TV show was enough of a distraction, now we need several). Or checking my phone when I'm with Christiane, or when the children are trying to get my attention. OK, this sucks for them, but it's me who is really missing out. Instead of beating myself up about this, I take a breath, put my phone down and spend time really being with the people I love.

So this mindless addiction to phones is the opposite of mindfulness. Mindfulness is living in the moment – enjoying and savouring the experience you're having right at that moment. Not thinking about the past, or the future, or what's going on somewhere else, but that moment, right then and there. Our addiction to phones is getting in the way. It makes us not at all present for our loved ones – we're not savouring the moment and our mind is elsewhere, which is very sad.

So what should you do? Well I'm sure your phone is important. You need it in case your boss emails you asking you to do something urgent or important. Or in case your child's school calls to say they're poorly… or if one of the Kardashians wears a new bikini, and so on. Sometimes you need to check in with your phone and that's fine. But let go of mindlessly browsing on it when you don't need to. Have a set time to check your emails – say, once every hour or two. Or devote an hour of your evening to sitting down after dinner and going through your emails. Then put your phone in another room and ignore it. Or if you can't do that, put it on a coffee table in front of you so that it's out of reach but you can see if somebody calls you. Do the same if you're out to dinner or drinks with friends – if you can, put your phone in your pocket or bag. If not, put it on the table, but don't touch it for the entire time unless somebody calls or texts you and it's vital that you answer it (it almost never is). Then, instead of falling down the rabbit hole of social media, emails and mindless online information, spend time focusing on, and talking to, your friends and loved ones. I remember I was speaking with a friend just after my father passed away. As I was sharing my feelings, he picked up his phone and started checking social media – I'm sure he didn't mean to be so hurtful, in fact it was a 'mindless' act rather than a malicious one. But it also fractured our friendship. Trust me, people notice if you're always on your phone when they're trying to talk to you. Be the kind of person that makes people feel special and listened to. Put. Your. Phone. Down.

The other time many of us turn to our phones is right before bed – and this doesn't work for many reasons. Firstly, the blue light emitted from most phones stimulates our brains and disrupts our quality of sleep. A 2015 Norwegian study found that people who spend time looking at their phones or tablets before bed take longer to fall asleep, will sleep less and feel less rested when they wake up. Anyone familiar with my previous books will know that sleep is a vital part of living Clean and Lean.

When they come to see me, many of my new clients aren't getting enough sleep. In the past this was usually down to working too hard, going out too much or just being stressed, which was stopping them from falling asleep or keeping them awake in the night. Now it's their phones keeping them awake – and this is really bad news for our health.

'MINDFULNESS REQUIRES DISCIPLINE. I SLIP UP ALL THE TIME, BUT EVERY NOW AND THEN I CHECK MYSELF'

When we sleep, our hormones restore themselves, including the ones that regulate our appetites and fat-burning. So sleep deprivation can make us hungrier and less able to burn fat. Well that sucks. It also makes us crave the wrong types of things, such as excess caffeine to keep us awake and processed sugar to provide us with a quick hit of energy. This puts us into a cycle of jittery highs and crashing lows and disrupts our sleep even further (caffeine or sugar after lunch can disrupt sleep later that evening). Plus it causes weight gain around the stomach and waist area, and even on your calves – when you're not producing optimal amounts of human growth hormone (which is produced while you sleep), fat is often stored on the calves. Lastly, being sleep deprived makes you less mindful in general because it leaves you tired, grumpy and unable to concentrate.

But here's the good news – it's often a really easy fix. Put your phone to bed two hours before you do. In fact, when was the last time you actually switched your phone off? Scary, right? Do what I now do and turn your phone off for at least an hour (try two hours, if you can) before bed. And instead of spending that time staring into your phone, falling down that rabbit hole of mindless internet browsing, ignoring your partner and generally wiring your brain up for a bad night's sleep, spend it talking to your partner. Or do some stretching and breathing exercises. Or have a warm, oily bath, or read a book (reading a book on an electronic device stimulates your brain in a way that reading a physical book doesn't).

2 Exercise mindfully

It's not just eating mindlessly that can damage your health – you can also exercise mindlessly and, therefore, very dangerously. People who exercise mindlessly tend to exercise because they feel they should. They are often driven by a lack of self-acceptance, which is why they may go to classes where they push their body beyond exhaustion while an underpaid egomaniac screams, 'Feel the burn!' No sane person that actually thought about it would think dancing around in a hot room for 90 minutes a day could actually be good for you. Yet many people do because some celebrity who along with the trainer, make millions from other people's misery and injuries, pretends it works for them. If it sounds crazy and hurts you, then you're doing the wrong thing. If you're counting the minutes until you can leave, you probably need to find another form of exercise. To exercise mindfully is to really connect with how your body is moving. This has two main benefits – one, you'll enjoy exercise more, which will make you exercise more, which will improve your health and fitness. Secondly, studies show that when you focus on the exercises you're doing and really think about your muscles as you're working them, the muscles work harder – it actually increases the neural flow. You get better results because you're focused on your posture, breathing, movement and form. Pounding away on a treadmill while watching TV won't get the same results as a focused 30 minutes thinking about how straight your back is, how strong your lungs feel, or how hard you can feel your muscles working all over your body.

3 Take a tip from children

This advice is inspired by watching my own children, Charlotte and Leo. There are two benefits that children have over adults when it comes to being mindful – their sleep and their attitude. Let's start with their sleep. Try to give yourself the kind of bedtime routine a child has. Don't wet the bed and start crying – I know from personal experience that stops being cute when you turn 30. Take Charlotte for example. Every single night, pretty much without fail, she has her dinner, a bath and then a story. This bedtime ritual helps her fall asleep deeply because it's so ingrained in her day. Just hearing the taps run for her bath puts her into wind-down mode and sleepiness starts to slowly kick in.

After her bath and book we suggest she takes a few deep breaths, which calm her down further. Then we have a little chat about her day and ask her what parts of it she's grateful for – which can range from a trip to the park or a particularly tasty dinner. This helps her to be mindful and connect with what's going on around her. It calms her mind and she falls asleep very easily when we finally put her to bed. I can imagine that this routine may sound unrealistic (and perhaps a little annoying?). A bit like when celebrities write cookbooks and advise you to sing to your cucumbers and massage your tomatoes. But the truth is, it's easy and it's worth it. Compare it to how the average adult goes to sleep – myself included sometimes. We have dinner, watch TV, spend two or three hours on our brightly lit mobile phones (remember – the backlight of most phones wires our brain in a way that disrupts sleep) and then we collapse, exhausted, into bed. But by then, despite having been sleepy all evening, we lie awake feeling tired, but wired, and unable to sleep. Sound familiar?

So if we take a tip from children, having a bedtime routine will increase your mindfulness, reduce your stress levels and improve your sleep quality. Wind down before bed. Take a few moments or minutes to think about and process your day, avoid your phone and get to bed well before the clock strikes midnight.

The second thing we can take from children is their wonderful ability to live in the moment. Children don't worry about the past or the future, they just exist in the moment. Of course, they have that luxury – they don't have the worries or responsibilities of adults, like job or money issues, or getting chores done, or all the other things adults worry about. But worries aside, we can all take a tip from children and just be mindful and in the moment. So now when I'm playing with them, I'm just enjoying that time – I'm not thinking about the phone in my pocket, or what I've got to do tomorrow. I'm right there with them. And I try to do the same when I'm with Christiane or my friends – I enjoy the moment and I don't let other stuff get in my mind.

Children also find wonder in everything – a tree bowing in the breeze, a clump of flowers in the grass, a bird or plane flying overhead. They point and stare and look amazed. Whereas adults tend to rush through life, too busy to notice all the beautiful little things around them. I realise that sounds a bit hippyish but we should all be a little more like children and notice the wonderful stuff that's happening around us every now and then, instead of being glued to our phones or rushing through life.

Lastly, children breathe in a very mindful way. They breathe in and their tummy expands, which is the ideal breath. It's a full, deep breath that's instantly calming. Adults, on the other hand, get out of the habit of doing this and tend to 'stress breathe', taking quick, shallow breaths. One of the best ways to be more mindful – and reduce stress levels – is to make sure you're breathing correctly. Shallow breathing has been shown to release the stress hormone cortisol, which makes us jittery (and increases fat storage around the mid section). While proper breathing reduces stress. So breathe in until first your tummy and then your chest fill and, as you slowly exhale, you'll feel calm. Take the time throughout a busy day to take a deep breath and you'll feel instantly calmer and more mindful.

> 'CHILDREN DON'T WORRY ABOUT THE PAST OR THE FUTURE. THEY JUST EXIST IN THE MOMENT'

4 *Accept stress*

Lastly, I want you to flip your thinking when it comes to stress. For years we've been taught to avoid stress – to walk away from a stressful relationship, or to quit a stressful job. Stress is bad – end it or avoid it, or so we've been told. But how about instead we just accept stress? You see, you will always experience stress in your life. You will always have a commute that just sucks – either your bus will be late, or your train will be cancelled (usually when it's raining or you have an important meeting with your boss). There'll be a traffic jam on the way to work, or you'll take a wrong turn and get lost. Certain people will annoy you and do selfish, stupid things. You'll spill coffee on your carpet or your child will break something or smear food on your sofa. Work will feel frustrating at times or your boss will annoy you. Stress is everywhere. So rather than trying to change the things causing you stress, why not change the way you deal with it? Simply accept it, breathe and move on. Accept that these annoying things are going to happen, but that they won't really matter years from now. So don't fight stress – simply see it coming, deal with it, and then send it on its way.

5 *Eat mindfully*

Do you eat while browsing on your phone, or at your desk at work? Do you eat out of boredom? Or because you're craving sugar? Do you turn to sugary foods when you're stressed or unhappy and do you often 'impulse eat' food that you're not even hungry for? For example, do you always order a muffin with your latte, or plate up some biscuits when you're making yourself a cup of tea? And will you often finish a large bag of crisps, without even realising until you see the bag is empty? If so, you're probably eating mindlessly. I fly frequently and I once got into the habit of buying salt and vinegar crisps and a Bounty bar every single time I got to the airport. This was serious business and I would eat that combination like it was my job. What was I thinking? I wasn't. I just somehow got into the habit and mindlessly continued until one day Chrissy and I were flying together and she asked me what I was doing. Well, she actually asked for two crisps and a bite of Bounty… but it got me thinking and I stopped this mindless habit.

Eating mindlessly is like every other mindless behaviour – it's done subconsciously, without thinking and without enjoying or savouring the moment (or in this case, the food). When you eat this way you tend to overeat, and reach for quick, processed junk food that gives you an initial – but often short-lived – high. Eating mindlessly can also cause problems for your digestion, because when you eat thoughtlessly, you tend to eat very quickly and not chew your food properly. Chewing is one of the best things you can do for your digestion – it releases all the vitamins and minerals in the food, and brings out the flavour in food, which helps you feel fuller quicker and increases your enjoyment of it. It also produces saliva that helps break food down and makes it easier for the stomach to digest. Half-chewed food sitting in your gut and eating too quickly can cause wind, bloating and burping. So eat and chew mindfully. It should take around 20 minutes to finish a meal.

How to eat MINDFULLY

Chew your food
Chew every mouthful of food around 10 to 20 times until it's a watery, mushy paste (please don't spit it out to check!).

Set aside time to eat
Do it away from your desk, TV, laptop and phone, and ideally at a table. If you really do have to eat at your desk, at the very least take a big deep breath before you eat and tune in to your body for 30 seconds. Then look for a new job.

Put your knife and fork down
Let your body recognise when it's full. Eating quickly and mindlessly causes you to miss the signs that you are full and you overeat as a result.

Don't eat when you're stressed
Stress is a major cause of mindless eating, so if you're anxious or bothered about something, take a few deep breaths, go for a walk or tackle the situation before you eat. Don't confuse stress with hunger.

Are you looking for food because you're hungry, or because you need a break from your surroundings?

Buy food mindfully
Don't just buy the same things week in week out. Try different things, visit local food markets, independent butchers and greengrocers. Ask them what they recommend and find out what's seasonal, what looks and smells the best. Think about how you're going to cook it and connect with what you're putting into your body.

Prepare food mindfully
Try new recipes and experiment with new cooking methods (read more about this in chapter 3).

Listen to your body and stop when you're full
Forget the 'clean your plate' message your mum or teacher may have imposed and don't be afraid to leave food on your plate. Don't mindlessly eat it just because it's there.

Try these mindful, 'LESS-STRESS' FOODS

Avocados

They help to lower blood pressure and, because they're creamy and full of filling good fats, they put a swift end to mid-afternoon hunger pangs.

Beetroot

This also helps to lower blood pressure and is packed with health-boosting vitamins.

Berries

These are perfect snack foods because they're sweet (so satisfy a sugar craving) but they're also full of vitamin C, which helps the body deal with stress and boosts overall health and immunity, as well as fibre.

Nuts

Like avocados, they contain good fats so are very filling. They're also full of B vitamins, which help reduce stress. Just be careful not to mindlessly overeat. If you eat mindfully – which means chewing them properly and slowly – and savour them, you're less likely to eat too many.

Turkey

Turkey meat releases calming hormones like serotonin and can even help give you a better nights sleep. It's also a lovely Clean and Lean food because it's natural and nourishing with no added nasties.

'THE BENEFITS OF MINDFUL EATING INCLUDE A FLATTER STOMACH, FEWER DIGESTIVE COMPLAINTS AND WEIGHT LOSS'

WE EAT 50%
MORE FOOD
WHEN WE EAT IN
FRONT OF THE
TV ACCORDING
TO A STUDY
FROM CORNELL
UNIVERSITY IN
NEW YORK.

Here are other ways to be more mindful with your workouts:

1 Change things around

If you always run, try yoga once a week. If you love aerobics, try lifting weights. Don't get stuck in a fitness rut. This also helps you use more muscle groups and trains your body in a different way, which will help you lose weight, look lean and, most importantly, feel amazing.

2 Have a goal to focus on – and reassess it regularly

Set yourself mini goals. At the start that might just be to get fit or get ready for a 5k fun run. Then reassess that goal. Do you want to run 10k, or learn how to dance, play tennis, achieve a physical challenge like a pull up (or ten), a hand stand, or get better posture? Whatever it is, have fun with it!

3 Be good, not fast

Don't rush through your workouts. Good posture and form are far better and more beneficial than speed, so take your time and think about all your movements.

4 Breathe better

Try to take deep, full breaths that will keep you in the moment, flood your body with lovely energising oxygen and help you achieve more.

5 Stretch

It sounds obvious, but always stretch well after a work out. As well as being very good for your muscles and posture, it helps you to be mindful of the muscles you've worked and what you've achieved. It may also help reduce cortisol (the stress hormone), which will help you let go of fat at the front of your tummy.

6 Remind yourself of the truth – your body loves to move

Rather than seeing exercise as a chore that needs to be squeezed in between work and whatever else you need to do, see it for what it really is, a way of making you feel amazing – something that gives you more energy throughout the day, that will help protect you against all sorts of illnesses, strengthen your bones and help you sleep better. Your body loves to move, so move it every day.

7 Don't worry if you don't like the gym

So many people think they either have to go to the gym after work or sit on their sofa and eat junk. But there's a lovely middle ground and it's called movement. Your body is designed to move a lot, but work or life often get in the way. So every chance you get, move your body and it will thank you for it. Walk as much as you can, potter about, run around with your children, play tennis, or football, or netball with your friends. Go on long walks at the weekend and stay active. You are so lucky to have a healthy, active body so cherish it and move it as much as possible.

chapter 3

HOW TO COOK CLEAN AND LEAN

You can never be
TOO PREPARED

To be Clean and Lean you need to know how to cook. But don't panic! You don't need to be a chef or have a state-of-the-art kitchen full of expensive gadgets. However, you do need to know the basics, because cooking from scratch is the quickest, easiest and healthiest way to become Clean and Lean. If you know the principles of Clean and Lean, but you're still relying on supermarket ready meals or pre-packaged soups (even healthy looking ones) you're still going to be getting a lot of sugar, additives and other nasties. The good news is, it's really easy – even I can do it!

Top tip!
Fresh lemons, though sour, add sweetness to desserts. They also make fish tender and add flavour to pretty much every dish, so always have a few in your fruit bowl ready to be sliced.

One of the biggest complaints I hear from my clients is that they don't have time to cook. I work with men and women who leave their desks at 6pm and get home at 7 or 8pm, too exhausted to make anything other than pasta or a ready meal. I work with mums who have to make all their meals with a 10-month-old on their hip. I get it. I have a 10-month-old. And a 3-year-old and a business and house to run. Cooking from scratch seems impossible when you look at it like that.

Which is why you need to prepare. You need containers in your fridge filled with chopped vegetables and stock. (You can make your own or you can get some great stock – much fresher than the ready-made kind – from your local butcher or grocers.) You need quick and easy flavours like garlic, ginger and fresh lemon, right by your cooker. You need olive oil and coconut oil in your kitchen at all times, along with a fridge full of vegetables and protein, like chicken, eggs, cheese, meat and fish. Now, before you start feeling inadequate about the contents of your fridge, you don't need all of these all the time. But it's good to have a handy supply of the essentials. And just remember, if all this sounds too expensive, know that your health is worth the investment and just do what you can with what you've got.

It sounds obvious but make sure you always have food in your house, because if you don't, you'll be tempted to call for a takeaway. Or buy a pizza (loaded with fake, funky flavours and white flour) on your way home and put it in the oven. Or you'll tip a load of pasta in a pan. You know it's not Clean and Lean but you're tired and you can't face heading to the shop to buy some proper food. So ALWAYS stock your cupboards, fridge and freezer with Clean and Lean food so you can throw something together quickly and easily. Once it becomes a habit it will be much easier. Please remember, you deserve to feel good and these simple habits will help you achieve that.

What to keep in YOUR KITCHEN

Clean and Lean FLAVOURS

If you add your own Clean flavours to your dishes you won't need to rely on the fake, sugary alternatives you find in shop-bought (and factory made) salad creams, dressings, marinades and ketchup. Clean flavours also bring out the natural flavours in meat and vegetables, making them even tastier, which makes becoming Clean and Lean even more enjoyable.

* Basil-infused olive oil
* Garlic-infused olive oil
* Coconut oil
* Extra virgin olive oil (the best you can buy)
* Flaxseed oil
* Sesame oil
* Walnut oil
* White wine vinegar
* Chillies
* Dijon mustard
* Fresh mayonnaise such as Delouis Fils (keep refrigerated)
* Lemons
* Limes
* Tamari soy sauce (gluten-free and can be used instead of salt)
* Coriander
* Dill
* Parsley
* Thyme

Clean and Lean PROTEINS

Don't feel like you need to have meat every day. It's far healthier (and cheaper) to buy good-quality, organic, locally reared meat from your local butcher and enjoy it once or twice a week rather than bulk-buying cheap meat at the supermarket and having it every single day. And be mindful about your meat – if you can buy two whole chickens for £5, question the quality of that meat and the integrity of the farming methods involved.

* Beef
* Chicken
* Duck
* Lamb
* Liver
* Turkey
* Fish and shellfish (to limit mercury, just stick to one serving of tuna or swordfish a week)

You'll notice there's no pork in this list. Someone once told me that pigs are as intelligent, if not more so, than dogs. And I once watched a pig happily roll around in its own poo for 30 minutes. So I just can't bring myself to eat pork or recommend it. I know that there are lots of angry vegans (I love you by the way and I thank you for helping save the world with your choices) who will accuse me of being a hypocrite because I recommend eating other animals. I have no excuse and no leg to stand on. You're right. But essentially I just want people to choose more kindly and less cruelly. Go for free range and ask about the treatment of the animals. As I have become more mindful I am finding I eat less meat and choose it far more discerningly. True change comes through inspiration rather than shame and guilt. Anyway, I'm trying my best, so please read on!

I especially LOVE...

Cinnamon
This is one of my favourite Clean flavours. It helps keep your blood sugar levels steady, which reduces sugar cravings, and it also acts as an anti-inflammatory so it can help with aches and pains. You can sprinkle it on your coffee (use this in the place of sugar for Clean sweetness) or add it to desserts.

Garlic
I love garlic more than anything. It adds delicious Clean flavour to almost any dish, it's antiviral, an antioxidant and is great for your heart health and immunity. It also helps the healthy bacteria in your gut to thrive. So add whole cloves to casseroles or slice it into stir-fries or crush it up to really bring out the flavour.

Rosemary
Rosemary has been used for centuries to boost your mood. Add it to salads, stir fries and lamb dishes. It has also been said to be a blood cleanser and that's kind of amazing.

Sage
This is a fantastic purifier, antioxidant and anti-inflammatory. It's also good for indigestion.

Turmeric
This bright yellow herb is an incredible anti-inflammatory and can be used for muscle and joint pain. It's also a very powerful antioxidant and great for your liver. Watch this one – it will be the new celebrity ingredient in the coming years – so get in now!

Clean and Lean
VEGETABLES

Still not convinced about organic fruits and vegetables? Remember, they contain twice as many vitamins as non-organic ones, and the more nutrients your body consumes, the less hungry it feels and the less it wants sugar. If you can't afford organic, head to your local greengrocers instead – the fruit and veg there is likely to be locally sourced so it'll contain less toxic preservatives. This is why the tomatoes you buy locally go off quickly, while the ones you buy in your big local supermarket stay hard, red and shiny for weeks and weeks. Remember, be mindful of your food – question what's keeping them that way? And while we're on the organic versus pesticide-sprayed debate, there are piles of research to support both, so for me it comes down to simple common sense. If something is sprayed with poisons that even bugs won't eat, then surely something that hasn't been sprayed with this stuff is better, right?

* Asparagus
* Avocado
* Broccoli
* Brussels sprouts
* Courgette
* Cucumber
* Green beans
* Kale
* Mushrooms
* Mangetout
* Onions
* Sweet peppers
* Rocket
* Spinach
* Sweet potatoes
* Watercress

Clean and Lean
EGGS, MEAT AND DAIRY

It's especially important to buy organic meat, eggs and dairy. However, if you can't afford it take this top tip – always remove the skin from non-organic meat (like chicken) because that's where most of the toxins are stored. And if you don't buy organic fruits and vegetables, scrub and wash them well before cooking or eating. It takes two minutes so yes, you do have time.

Top tip!
Just about any vegetable is Clean and Lean. Remember – have something green every day (ideally with every meal).

Clean and Lean
NUTS AND SEEDS

Eat raw nuts whenever possible – the roasting process can increase free-radical damage in your body. Or roast them yourself with a little Clean flavour added.

* Almonds
* Brazil nuts
* Cashews
* Chestnuts
* Macadamias
* Pecans
* Pistachios
* Flaxseeds
* Walnuts
* Linseed (ground only)
* Peanuts
* Pumpkin seeds
* Sesame seeds
* Sunflower seeds
* Chia seeds

How to be CLEAN and LEAN in the KITCHEN

1 Don't be afraid to experiment – or make mistakes

There is no right or wrong way to cook (within reason). So have fun with it and never be afraid to experiment. If you want to cook one of the recipes in the following chapters but it uses a flavour or ingredient you don't like, just leave that ingredient out or substitute it with something else. See recipes as a guide, not as a set of rules. Once you master one or two recipes you can then tweak them and start swapping flavours or ingredients around. You don't need to be a chef to be a good cook. Chrissy and I aren't chefs. We're not trained in cooking but we know how to put food together that tastes great and keeps us healthy. I have no idea what I'm doing half the time, but I do know what tastes great, so I throw in a lot of my favourite things and see what happens. One of the nicest emails I got after the first Clean and Lean book came out was from a lady who said, 'Thank goodness – a book that doesn't require a degree in cooking!' So keep cooking fun. That way you'll see it as something enjoyable rather than a tiresome chore you need to do quickly.

2 Be mindful

I talked about this in the previous chapter, but it never hurts to be reminded. So when it comes to cooking, be mindful. Think about the ingredients you're using – how do they smell, feel and taste? Are they fresh? Are they real? Or do they have a weird, toxic, fake smell and appearance (if so ditch them for something Clean). Don't rush through the process of cooking. Enjoy it, savour it, get involved and be in the moment. Even the simple act of food preparation can become a lovely experience if you're mindful about it.

3 Get the family involved

Get the family involved in cooking. Most evenings Charlotte and I cook together. She's three but she can do basic stuff like sniffing the herbs and spices and then sprinkling them in the pan if she approves. This is such an amazing way to connect with her and if you have children I beg you to try it. It also gives her a deeper appreciation of food and a connection with the very thing that's keeping her healthy, strong and alive. I hope it helps her relationship with food and health in the future. I put my phone down and we get stuck in.

4 Feed your kids how you feed yourself

Lots of parents make themselves eggs for breakfast (very Clean and Lean) and then give their children a bowl of sugary cereal (not at all Clean and Lean). Why is that? Why not just all eat the same? One reason is the food manufacturers have made a very nice living from telling parents that their children need sugary cereal with various health claims on the packet. The truth is, children should be eating the same food as adults (as long as it's age appropriate and mushed up enough if they're really young). Take my breakfast for example – I love putting oats, nuts and seeds in a bowl, topping it with almond or rice milk and letting it soak overnight. In the morning I sprinkle a handful of berries and some chia seeds on top. Charlotte loves it! Obviously you need to be careful with seeds or anything that small children can choke on. And please don't ever say, 'But all they'll eat is cereal', because that's a cop out. Don't buy it in the first place – your two-year-old doesn't order the online grocery shop on the internet or walk to the shop themselves. Be a loving guardian of what they experience and eat.

5 Make too much of everything

Whenever you're making food, make too much. Then put the leftovers in the fridge for tomorrow's breakfast, lunch or dinner. This also helps with the 'I'm too busy to eat properly' dilemma.

6 Keep it simple

Recipes can sometimes have just one or two ingredients. I often take an apple, bake it and then add a spoonful of Greek yogurt. It's so simple. My meals are made in the cauldron of real life busy. I don't always have 10 hours to boil bones (in case you didn't know, making your own bone broth is a thing now, see page 100). I don't have lots of time to cook – I want quick and simple meals, as I'm sure you do. By the way – if you do have time, bone broths are amazing. So if you can, go for it!

7 Invest in some labour-saving gadgets

OK, I know I said at the start of this chapter that you don't need a state-of-the-art kitchen with lots of fancy gadgets but if you can afford it, there are a few things that will make life more fun (and healthy) in the kitchen. A blender is a great addition because you can make smoothies, juices, sauces and dips with it. I also love griddle pans – there's something about griddling a vegetable that enhances its flavour, and I also love making an omelette and then gently griddling it. Get griddling people! Lastly, if you can afford it, get a spiraliser (at the time of writing they cost around £10 to £20, so much cheaper than a blender). You may have heard a lot about them recently because they've become hugely popular. Well, they're basically gadgets that turn vegetables into noodles. Soft, easy to slice vegetables like courgettes are very easy to spiralise, or you could try sweet potato, or even apples. The fruit or vegetable has to be slightly tough to work though – a banana is too soft and would just mush up. Then you can add these 'noodles' to stir fries or top them with meatballs and sauces rather than having pasta.

8 Make it slowly

Another good tip for people too busy to cook in the evenings is to put your meal on before you leave the house. This is also good for weekends or when you've got a lot of friends coming over for dinner and you don't want to spend all your time in the kitchen. I often put meals in my slow cooker or in a large casserole dish and put them in the oven for seven or eight hours. One of my favourite recipes is lamb shoulder, chopped leeks, sweet potatoes, rosemary, garlic, onions and any other vegetables I have lying around, thrown in a casserole dish with a little bit of stock, covered and left to cook slowly. It takes less than 20 minutes to prepare and it's amazing. When you take it out of the oven the lamb falls off the bone and is so tender. My other favourite is a simple chicken covered, stuffed and rubbed with coconut oil, lemons and garlic. Make these and you can thank me later.

Top tip!
Chop up a few vegetables on a Sunday night and put them in sealable containers in the fridge. They can then be added to soups, stir fries and casseroles for some lovely Clean flavour throughout the week.

Clean ways to cook

1 Baking

This simply involves cooking food in your oven in a dry heat. If you add water and stock and lots of clean flavour (like lemons, garlic, herbs and spices) and cook for a long period of time, your meat will be incredibly tender and full of flavour from the foods surrounding it. Delicious. Look out for my Lamb Summer Stew (see page 167).

2 Blanching

This keeps vegetables crisp and nutritious. Boil them for a minute or two, then remove from the water, drain, and plunge in a bowl of icy water. Then quickly boil them again for a minute just before serving. Blanche is also a lovely name for a lady.

3 Frying

This has a bad reputation, but frying can be a lovely way to cook Clean and Lean foods. Simply heat a little coconut oil and throw in all your food (like chicken and vegetables). The same goes for an omelette. The key to keeping frying Clean and Lean is to use the right oil and to not over-fry. You want the meat or fish just cooked through.

4 Grilling

This is a lovely, quick and healthy way to cook meat, fish and vegetables that retains a lot of goodness but also enhances the flavour. This is a personal favourite of mine.

5 Steaming

This way of cooking retains the most nutrients, goodness and flavour in your fish, meat, fruits or vegetables. You can either buy a steamer (don't buy a microwave one – in my opinion, microwaves cook food in a way that destroys much of the goodness – hi microwave people, I look forward to your annual threatening letter!) or put the food in a sieve over a pan of boiling water with a lid on top.

> **Top tip!**
> Don't heat olive oil – use it cold drizzled over salads. If you need an oil to cook with use coconut oil instead.

How NOT to cook

1 Don't microwave your protein

In fact, try not to microwave anything because microwaving really concerns me. Microwaves can alter the molecular structure of protein, leaving it unrecognisable to your gut wall and causing inflammation.

2 Never overcook meat

If you overcook meat, you lose so much flavour and also many wonderful nutrients. However, always cook chicken thoroughly and until piping hot in the middle because of the risk of food poisoning.

3 Never blacken or char your meat or fish

Especially when barbecuing food. The black stuff you often see on barbecued food is harmful to your system.

4 Don't over-boil your vegetables

You'll retain more of the vitamins if you lightly steam (not in the microwave), boil or roast your vegetables.

5 Don't get stressed

There are bigger problems in the world than a burnt roast. If you make something and it doesn't turn out right, just try again tomorrow. Don't lose sight of the fact that you want to be Clean and Lean – because you deserve to be. It is a process and a journey that will inform the rest of your life. So enjoy your new, amazing healthy life and don't stress about the odd hiccup en route.

Evening snacking

If you work from home and tend to graze, or if you often find yourself snacking in the evening, try these ideas for Clean snacks.

Make your own granola

Get some buckwheat, oats, quinoa flakes, toasted coconut, pumpkin seeds, your favourite nuts, coconut palm sugar and coconut oil, mix it all up and sprinkle it with cinnamon and Himalayan salt. Make a big batch that you can dip into throughout the week. It tastes great dry or you can add a couple of dollops of coconut yogurt or almond milk and a sprinkling of fruit for a quick breakfast.

Sweet and sour nuts

Spread your favourite nuts out on a baking tray, sprinkle them with a little cinnamon or tamari sauce and bake them for approximately 10 minutes.

Jazz up some fruit

This is so simple but seriously good. Make some almond butter (it's so easy, I promise – see page 200 for the recipe) and spread some on apple slices or celery sticks.

Serenity Sleep

This is my favourite night-time snack. Buy a pack of the Clean and Lean Serenity supplement and mix a scoop into Greek or coconut yogurt and sprinkle with berries. The ingredients in Serenity include chamomile, hops and barley which will get you nice and relaxed for a wonderful night's sleep.

A word about
JUICING

When I wrote the first Clean and Lean book I used to make my own juices and smoothies every day. Back then this was something only a few people – usually working in fitness or nutrition – did. Now, everybody is at it. Juice bars are the new coffee bars and you're just as likely to see a juice on the menu at your local café as you are a coffee. Equally it's as common to see somebody walking down the road clutching a juice, as a latte. I still love juicing, but you have to know a few things in order to make it work for, and not against you. Rather than going to extremes and living on nothing but liquid for days at a time, I opt for a vegetable-based juice as a mid-morning or afternoon snack. Juices aren't a nourishing enough option for breakfast as they will not set you up for the day or give you the energy you deserve.

A word about
SMOOTHIES

Smoothies are a really intelligent and delicious way of nourishing yourself in today's fast-paced world and a great quick breakfast option. I use my blender most mornings to mix up lots of green vegetables with a scoop of the Clean and Lean Body Brilliance supplement, a handful of berries, some nuts and sometimes some

Top tip!
Lukewarm juice isn't great, so always add ice to your smoothies and juices. Nothing makes a green juice more palatable than a handful of ice.

coconut yogurt too. If you're blending apples, berries and melon with only a tiny bit of kale, you're not doing it right. All that fruit will provide a huge hit of sugar – fructose, which is a naturally occurring fruit sugar, but it's still sugar and you can still have too much of it. So always add a bit of fruit to a lot of vegetables and some good fats. Remember the basic Clean and Lean principles and you'll be fine. The reality is we don't always have time to sit down to a lovingly prepared breakfast or lunch, but we do have time to throw together a smoothie that will create the foundation for a healthy, happy day or a nourishing health boost to keep you going.

chapter 4

Breakfasts

DELICIOUS DIGESTION BOOSTING GRANOLA *Serves 4–6*

Ingredients

255g gluten-free oats or flakes of
any variety (such as quinoa, brown
rice, millet)
170g raw buckwheat groats
130g pumpkin seeds
1½ teaspoons ground cinnamon
1½ teaspoons ground ginger
1 teaspoon vanilla extract
225g coconut palm sugar
½ teaspoon salt
3 tablespoons coconut oil, melted
almond milk, to serve (optional)
mixed berries, to serve (optional)

Method

1. Preheat the oven to 180°C/gas mark 4. Line a baking tray with greaseproof paper.

2. Mix together the oats, buckwheat, pumpkin seeds, ground cinnamon, ground ginger and vanilla extract.

3. Put the coconut palm sugar and salt in a saucepan with 125ml water and heat slowly until the sugar has dissolved and has a syrupy texture.

4. Add the coconut oil and coconut palm sugar syrup to the dry ingredients and mix well.

5. Pour the granola onto the baking tray and use a spatula to flatten the mixture down so that it is about 1cm thick.

6. Bake for about 30 minutes, until golden brown and crisp. Leave to cool on the tray before storing in an airtight container. Enjoy with almond milk and a sprinkling of berries.

CACAO, CAROB AND COCONUT GRANOLA *Serves 4–6*

Cacao is the real deal – the untouched purest form of chocolate without all the sugary rubbish and it provides a great source of health-boosting antioxidants. Carob contains as much vitamin B1 as asparagus or strawberries and is packed with calcium, and coconut is a fantastic source of good fat which helps you metabolise bad fat.

Ingredients

300g coconut flakes, unsweetened
200g mixed nuts
50g pumpkin seeds
30g sunflower seeds
30g cacao nibs
3 tablespoons chia seeds
1 tablespoon raw cacao powder
1 teaspoon carob powder
1 teaspoon ground cinnamon
3 tablespoons maple syrup
4 tablespoons coconut oil, melted

Method

1. Preheat the oven to 150°C/gas mark 2. Line 2 baking trays with baking paper and set aside.

2. Put all the dry ingredients into a large bowl and mix to combine. Once thoroughly mixed, stir in the wet ingredients.

3. Lay the granola out evenly on the baking trays trying not to have any ingredients on top of each other.

4. Bake for 10–15 minutes, or until golden brown, then remove from the oven and leave to cool completely before storing in an airtight jar for up to 2 weeks. (The oil may sink to the bottom of the jar.)

APPLE, GINGER AND BLUEBERRY MUFFINS *Makes 12*

Chrissy's favourite snack or breakfast on-the-go is a fluffy muffin. She loves to satisfy her sweet tooth without falling off the Clean and Lean track and these fruity muffins do just that.

Ingredients

1 sweet eating apple, such as Pink Lady, peeled, cored and chopped
1 teaspoon ground cinnamon
210ml maple syrup
150g buckwheat flour
150g oats
2 teaspoons ground ginger
2 teaspoons vanilla extract
1 teaspoon baking powder
1 teaspoon bicarbonate of soda
½ teaspoon ground cinnamon
¼ teaspoon nutmeg
¼ teaspoon sea salt
2 free-range eggs
125ml almond milk
1 punnet blueberries
Greek or coconut yogurt, to serve

Method

1. Preheat the oven to 180°C/gas mark 4. Line a 12-hole muffin tray with muffin cases.

2. Put a saucepan over a medium heat and add the apple, cinnamon, 1 tablespoon of the maple syrup and 2 tablespoons water and stir. Cook until softened, about 20 minutes. Mash with a fork.

3. Meanwhile, put the flour, oats, ginger, 1 teaspoon of the vanilla extract, the baking powder, bicarbonate of soda and salt into a mixing bowl and stir well to combine. Add the eggs, almond milk and the remaining maple syrup and mix well. Fold in the apple mixture and then the blueberries.

4. Divide the mixture evenly between the muffin cases. Bake for about 20 minutes, or until a toothpick inserted in the centre comes out almost clean. Remove from the oven, leave to cool in the tray for 5 minutes and then transfer to a wire rack.

5. Enjoy with a spoonful of Greek or coconut yogurt.

COCONUT AND CACAO CLUSTERS *Serves 8–10*

Ingredients

255g organic oats
130g shredded coconut
115g maple syrup
115g honey
85g coconut oil
85g cacao nibs
½ teaspoon ground cinnamon
3 tablespoons white chia seeds
2 tablespoons water

Method

1. Preheat the oven to 180°C/gas mark 4. Line a tray with baking paper. Put all the dry ingredients, except for the chia, into a mixing bowl and mix together.

2. Melt the coconut oil, honey and maple syrup in a small pan over a low heat until just melted. Pour into the dry ingredients and mix thoroughly. Mix the chia with the water in a small bowl and stir. Combine with the rest of the ingredients until mixed. Now spread the oat mix onto the tray, pushing it down so it is packed tightly.

3. Cook for 15–20 minutes, or until golden brown. Remove from the oven and leave to cool for a few minutes. Now carefully lift the baking paper out of the tray and onto a wire rack and leave to cool completely.

4. Once properly cool and set, break up the clusters into chunks.

YOGURT *Serves 12*

Ingredients
2 litres whole milk
75g yogurt containing active
cultures

Equipment
cooking thermometer

Method
1. Put a small pan over a medium-high heat. Add the milk and heat until just below boiling, 94°C, stirring gently to make sure the bottom doesn't scorch and the milk doesn't boil over. Let it cool until it is just hot to the touch.

2. Pour about a cup of the warm milk into a small bowl, add the yogurt and use a whisk to mix it together. Once it's smooth, whisk this mixture back into the pan of warm milk.

3. Now incubate the mixture for around 4–6 hours. This step requires patience as it's when the milk actually transforms into yogurt. The trick is to keep the milk at around 43°C. You can buy incubating equipment that will maintain a consistent temperature, but it's not necessary. Try incubating your yogurt in the oven by warming it to about 46°C, then switching it off and putting your yogurt inside. Alternatively, put the lid on a Dutch oven or saucepan with your milk inside and wrap the whole pot in a few layers of tea towels. These will insulate the pot and keep it warm. It's important not to touch the yogurt as it's incubating so that it sets properly. The longer it sits, the thicker and tastier it will be. Check it at around the 4-hour mark and give it a taste – it should be creamy and tangy. Sometimes there will be a film of watery whey on top of the yogurt. You can strain this off or just stir it back in.

4. Once your yogurt is set you need to chill it. You can add compote (ideally using seasonal fruit) at this point to give it a delicious flavour. It will last for about 2 weeks in an airtight container in the fridge.

BAKED APPLE AND CINNAMON OATMEAL *Serves 4*

Ingredients
150g gluten-free oats
500ml almond milk
4 eating apples, chopped
4 teaspoons ground cinnamon
5 tablespoons raw honey
juice of 1 lemon
50g raisins
a handful of flaked almonds
a handful of goji berries
2 tablespoons almond butter
1 teaspoon vanilla extract

Method
1. Put the oats and the almond milk in a bowl and leave to soak.

2. Preheat the oven to 180°C/gas mark 4.

3. Put the apples, 1 teaspoon of the ground cinnamon, 1 tablespoon of the honey and all the lemon juice in a saucepan with a ladleful of water. Cook over a low heat until the apple has softened.

4. Mix all the other ingredients together.

5. Once the apples have cooked, add them to the mixture and then tip onto a baking tray and spread into an even layer. Bake for 15 minutes. Preheat the grill to medium-high, or switch the oven to the grill setting.

6. Grill for 5 minutes so the porridge gets a little crispy on top.

7. Serve with a spoonful of coconut yogurt and a sprinkling of berries.

SUPER PORRIDGE *Serves 1*

If this porridge was a basketball team, it would be the greatest basketball team that ever lived. Cacao, goji berry, quinoa and bee pollen – each ingredient is an absolute star player. They work together to ensure you get the best, most nutrient dense start to your day possible.

Ingredients

170g quinoa
500ml almond milk
1 tablespoon raw cacao powder
2 tablespoons coconut oil
1 tablespoon nut butter
2 tablespoons maple or
coconut syrup
½ teaspoon carob powder
½ teaspoon cinnamon powder

For the topping

1 teaspoon bee pollen
2 tablespoons goji berries
2 tablespoons coconut yogurt
a handful of nuts

Method

1. Rinse the quinoa well and put it in a saucepan over a medium heat with double the amount of almond milk. Cook for about 10 minutes, until the grain unwraps itself but still has a slight crunch and the milk has been absorbed (add more milk if it absorbs before it has cooked). Drain and rinse well in cold water, then tip back into the dry saucepan.

2. Add the raw cacao powder, coconut oil, nut butter, maple or coconut syrup, carob powder and cinnamon powder. Stir to combine. This will keep in the fridge, without the toppings, for 4–5 days, so it's great to make at the start of the week.

3. Serve in a bowl with the topping ingredients.

BIRCHER MUESLI WITH APPLE AND RHUBARB COMPOTE *Serves 1–2*

If you can't find Vanilla Protein, it's fine to go without. Or at the very least please get a very good-quality protein powder that you trust (if it comes in a bucket and has a picture of a bulging muscle then do not go near it).

Ingredients
For the muesli

85g gluten-free oats
375ml almond milk
1 scoop Bodyism Vanilla Protein
Excellence
¼ teaspoon ground cinnamon
1 heaped teaspoon almond butter
desiccated coconut, to serve

For the compote

1 red apple, chopped
3 rhubarb stalks, chopped
¼ teaspoon ground cinnamon
¼ teaspoon ground nutmeg
1 tablespoon raw honey (optional)

Method

1. To make the muesli, put the oats, almond milk, Vanilla Protein Excellence and cinnamon in a bowl and mix thoroughly. Chill in the fridge for two hours or overnight.

2. To make the compote, put all the ingredients in a pan over a low heat and simmer until soft. The amount here will give you more than one portion size so store any extra in the fridge or freezer to use at a later date.

3. To serve spoon the muesli into a bowl and top with 2 tablespoons of the compote, the almond butter and a generous sprinkling of desiccated coconut.

OVERNIGHT CREAMY QUINOA *Serves 4*

Ingredients

500ml almond milk
170g quinoa
a handful of flaked almonds
a handful of cacao nibs
a handful of goji berries
2 scoops Bodyism Body Brilliance
2 tablespoons maple syrup
1 tablespoon ground cinnamon
1 teaspoon vanilla extract
4 tablespoons coconut yogurt,
to serve

For the compote

110g blueberries
125g strawberries, chopped
110g raspberries
1 tablespoon lemon juice
1 tablespoon stevia
2 teaspoons ground cinnamon

Method

1. To make the compote, put all the ingredients in a saucepan over a low heat with 250ml water. Leave to cook for about 20 minutes, stirring occasionally. Take off the heat and leave to cool.

2. Rinse and drain the quinoa. Bring the almond milk to the boil in a separate saucepan and add the quinoa. Reduce the heat to medium-low and leave to simmer for about 10–15 minutes, until the milk has been absorbed and the quinoa has cooked. Add some more milk if the quinoa needs more time to cook completely.

3. Take the quinoa off the heat and add the rest of the ingredients to the pan. Mix well and store in an airtight container overnight. Serve the next morning with a spoonful of the berry compote and some coconut yogurt.

PROTEIN PANCAKES *Serves 1*

Flex your muscles with these sweet tasting clean and lean pancakes. I love them – they make me smile like a celebrity on one of those dancing shows on television. Big, crazy smiles.

Ingredients

25g Bodyism Vanilla Protein
Excellence
25g ground flaxseeds
3 free-range eggs, lightly beaten
25ml almond or rice milk
½ teaspoon vanilla extract
1 teaspoon maple syrup (optional)
coconut oil or butter, for frying

Method

1. Add the dry ingredients to a medium-sized bowl and mix thoroughly.

2. In a smaller bowl, beat the eggs, milk and vanilla, then add the mixture to the dry ingredients. Let the mixture sit for about 20–30 minutes.

3. Melt a little butter in a medium-sized frying pan over a medium-hot heat. Pour about 4 tablespoons of the batter into the pan and swirl it around to make a flat pancake. Cook for about 2 minutes, or until the edge of the pancake is starting to brown and pull away from the edges of the pan. Flip the pancake and continue to cook for about 2 minutes, until the bottom is lightly brown and cooked through. Serve with a drizzle of maple syrup.

LEMON AND COCONUT CHIA PUDDING *Serves 1*

If you're a lover of lemon this is for you. There are endless variations you can make for your chia pudding – have a look at cleanandlean.com to get inspired.

Ingredients

250ml unsweetened almond milk/
coconut milk
2 tablespoons chia seeds
1 tablespoon desiccated coconut
1 tablespoon stevia or xylitol
1 tablespoon coconut yogurt
1 teaspoon ground cinnamon
1 teaspoon vanilla extract
zest of 1 lemon
1 tablespoon coconut chips
fresh berries, to serve

Method

1. Put all the ingredients except the coconut chips and berries into your jar or bowl. Mix very well and then leave to set in the fridge overnight.

2. When you're ready to serve, preheat the oven to 180°C/gas mark 4 and toast the coconut chips on a baking tray for a few minutes, making sure they don't burn.

3. Sprinkle the toasted chips over the pudding along with the berries and serve.

EGG, CHIA AND RAINBOW CHARD MUFFINS *Makes 8–10*

Rainbow chard is another superstar vegetable. Try and seek it out at your local farmer's market, it could be a fun way to spend the weekend for you and your friends! Only kidding – if you can't find it, then any other cruciferous vegetable will work too, such as kale, spinach, courgette or steamed broccoli.

Ingredients

1 small onion, finely diced
12 free-range eggs
115g good-quality hard cheese,
grated
70g rainbow chard, chopped
2 tablespoons chia seeds
zest of 1 lemon
sea salt and freshly ground
black pepper
coconut oil or butter, for frying
and greasing

Method

1. Preheat the oven to 180°C/gas mark 4 and grease a muffin pan with a little coconut oil or butter.

2. Heat a little oil in a small frying pan over a medium heat. Add the onions and a tiny pinch of salt and sweat the onions.

3. While the onions are softening, crack the eggs into a bowl and whisk until smooth. Add the cheese and stir it all together.

4. Once the onions are softened, add the chard and continue to cook until wilted, about 2 minutes. Tip the mixture into the eggs along with the chia seeds. Stir to combine.

5. Ladle the mixture into the greased muffin pans and bake for 15 minutes. Remove and let them cool in the pan for 5 minutes before transferring to a wire rack to cool completely.

Top tip!
If you need a 'breakfast on-the-go', clean an empty jam jar and rustle up your chia puddings straight into it. Store in the fridge overnight.

Top tip!
Chia seeds are packed
with omega 3 fatty
acids which help boost
brain and heart health.
Sprinkle on almost
any type of dish.

THE CUP OF LIFE *Serves 1*

I am completely in love with this breakfast smoothie because it arms me with everything I need to be able to go out and take the world by storm. This breakfast is like having a cheerleading squad cheering you on all day – you feel happy, light and motivated.

Ingredients

1 banana, chopped
250ml almond milk
1 scoop Bodyism Body Brilliance
2 tablespoons porridge oats
2 tablespoons chia seeds
a handful of fresh spinach
a handful of berries of your choice
3 ice cubes

Method

1. Put all the ingredients into a blender and whizz.
2. Pour into a cup and enjoy.

APPLE, PEAR AND ROSEMARY PANCAKES *Serves 4*

Ingredients

*1 apple, peeled, cored and cut into
8 segments*
*1 pear, peeled, cored and cut into
8 segments*
2 free-range eggs, lightly beaten
200ml almond milk or full fat milk
200ml cream or coconut milk
1 tablespoon coconut flour
55g butter
*1 rosemary sprig, leaves separated
and chopped*
*sea salt and freshly ground
black pepper*

Method

1. Put the apple and pear segments into a small bowl with a tiny pinch of salt and mix.

2. In another bowl mix your eggs, milk, cream and coconut flour. Season and whisk lightly.

3. Melt the butter in a non-stick frying pan over a medium heat and fry the apples and pears lightly with the rosemary leaves.

4. Once the fruit is beginning to turn golden, pour in the batter and swirl it around so that it spreads out evenly, covering all the fruit. Cook for about 2 minutes, or until the edge of the pancake is starting to brown and pull away from the edges of the pan. Flip the pancake and continue to cook for about 2 minutes, until the bottom is lightly brown and cooked through.

PUMPKIN PIKELETS *Serves 6–8*

For a savoury variation, eat these pikelets with butter instead of sugar and cinnamon. I also like to reserve the pumpkin seeds – put them on a baking tray, sprinkle them with paprika and sea salt and roast them at the same time as the pumpkin, then enjoy them later as an afternoon snack.

Ingredients

*1 small pumpkin (about 1kg),
deseeded but not peeled (you can
keep the seeds for toasting)*
2 tablespoons buckwheat
butter or coconut oil, for frying
a pinch of ground cinnamon
a pinch of coconut palm sugar
Himalayan pink salt
*cinnamon or maple syrup, to serve
(optional)*

Method

1. Preheat the oven to 180°C and line a baking tray with baking paper.

2. Put the pumpkin on the tray and sprinkle it with salt to draw out the liquid. You do not need oil as it makes the pumpkin soggy. Roast for about 20 minutes, or until the flesh is soft enough to mash. Remove from the oven.

3. Slice off and discard the skin and place the flesh in a bowl. Mash with a potato masher or stick blender until smooth, then mix in the flour.

4. Heat a small frying pan over a medium heat until hot. Add the butter or coconut oil and about 2 tablespoons of the pumpkin mixture to the pan to form a pikelet. You can use as much or as little mixture as you like depending on how big you want the pikelet to be.

5. Cook the pikelets in batches until golden brown on the outside and cooked but still soft inside, about 3–4 minutes.

6. Sprinkle with cinnamon and syrup or a spoon of yogurt, if desired.

SWEET SECRET GREEN MUFFINS *Makes 10*

This is for those veggie haters who need a sneaky way of getting their dose of greens.

Ingredients

550g courgette, grated
3 free-range eggs, beaten
50g coconut palm sugar
120ml coconut oil, melted, plus
extra for greasing
1 teaspoon vanilla extract
290g gluten-free flour
50g raisins
50g Brazil nuts, chopped
2 teaspoons bicarbonate of soda
2 teaspoons ground cinnamon
1 teaspoon ground nutmeg
a pinch of salt

Method

1. Preheat the oven to 180°C/gas mark 4. Line a 10-hole muffin tin with a little butter or coconut oil.

2. Put the courgette, eggs, coconut sugar, coconut oil and vanilla in a mixing bowl and stir to combine.

3. Put the remaining ingredients in another bowl and mix together, then add the courgette mixture and mix thoroughly.

4. Divide the mixture evenly between the muffin cases so that they are two-thirds full. Bake for about 20 minutes, or until a toothpick inserted in the centre comes out almost clean. Remove from the oven, leave to cool in the tray for 5 minutes and then transfer to a wire rack.

'YOU'VE BEEN A VERY NUTTY BOY' MUFFINS *Makes 8-10*

These can be frozen and make a great packed lunch addition.

Ingredients

1 courgette, chopped
70g kale, chopped
2 free-range eggs
50g gluten-free oats or
quinoa flakes
30g Brazil nuts
25g almonds
25g cashews
25g walnuts
1 scoop Bodyism Protein Powder
20g sunflower seeds
oil, for greasing

Method

1. Preheat the oven to 180°C/gas mark 4. Lightly grease a muffin tray with oil.

2. Put all the ingredients except for the seeds in a food-processor and blitz until just combined. Stir in the sunflower seeds.

3. Divide the mixture evenly between the muffin cases so that they are two-thirds full. Bake for about 20 minutes, or until a toothpick inserted in the centre comes out almost clean. Remove from the oven, leave to cool in the tray for 5 minutes and then transfer to a wire rack.

Top Tip!
Brazil nuts are one of the only naturally occurring sources of selenium, which is a cancer fighter.

EGG AND AVOCADO BAKE *Serves 2*

This is your brunch showstopper; two of our breakfast heroes. Plus it looks beautiful and tastes even better.

Ingredients
1 large avocado, halved and stoned
½ red or green chilli,
finely chopped
½ garlic clove, finely chopped
2 small free-range eggs
2 teaspoons Parmesan cheese
sea salt and freshly ground
black pepper

Method
1. Preheat the oven to 120°C/gas mark ½. Line a baking tray with foil.
2. Put the avocado halves on the lined baking tray and sprinkle with the chilli and garlic. Crack the egg inside the hole, then bake until the egg is cooked to your liking. Remove from the oven.
3. Sprinkle with the seasonings and enjoy.

SMASHED AVOCADO-FILLED MUSHROOMS *Serves 4*

Garlic has many powerful benefits for your body. If you are as worried as I am about getting 'garlic breath', my top tip is to make sure you cut it in half and take out the green shoot; you get just as much flavour without the smell (I saw that on a Jamie Oliver TV show).

Ingredients
4 large flat mushrooms, washed
1 tablespoon coconut oil, melted
2 garlic cloves, crushed
2 avocados, peeled and stoned
juice of 1 lemon
1 teaspoon paprika
1 tablespoon tahini
sea salt and freshly ground
black pepper
poached or scrambled eggs,
to serve

Method
1. Preheat the oven to 180°C/gas mark 4. Line a baking tray with foil.
2. Place the mushrooms on the baking tray. Mix the coconut oil with the crushed garlic cloves, season and mix together. Pour the garlic mixture over the mushrooms and bake for 20 minutes.
3. Meanwhile, mash the avocados and mix with the remaining garlic, the lemon juice, paprika and tahini, then stir well. Season to taste.
4. Once the mushrooms are cooked, spoon the smashed avocado into the caps. Serve with poached or scrambled eggs and you have a mighty breakfast on your hands!

Top Tip!
Garlic helps improve blood circulation and lower blood pressure.

SMOKED TROUT HASH *Serves 4-6*

When you've got the time, this is a great breakfast to rustle up. It's perfect if you've had a big workout session and are in need of a little extra energy. Potatoes are higher GI and a little more fattening than the sweet variety, so if you want, swap the starchier version for sweet potatoes.

Ingredients
For the hash
400g boiled potatoes, cubed
15g butter
100g boneless trout, flaked
25ml cream
1 garlic clove, finely chopped
¼ teaspoon cayenne pepper
2 teaspoons chopped fresh dill
1 shallot, finely chopped
sea salt and freshly ground
black pepper
olive oil, for frying
1 lemon, cut into wedges, to serve

For the dressing
2 tablespoons crème fraîche
2 teaspoons grated fresh
horseradish
a handful of fresh garlic chives,
snipped

Method
1. Heat a good splash of oil in a frying pan over a low heat and cook the potatoes until starting to brown, about 6–8 minutes.

2. Add the butter, flaked trout, cream, garlic, cayenne pepper and 1 teaspoon of the dill. Season to taste. Continue to cook for about 10 minutes, stirring every couple of minutes so the mixture doesn't stick.

3. Make the dressing by mixing the crème fraîche with the horseradish, chives and the remaining dill.

4. Serve the hash hot, with the dressing and lemon wedges on the side.

Top tip!
Try to find time to sit and savour your breakfast. Take a few deep breaths before you eat, enjoy it and make sure you chew it properly.

SPINACH AND AVOCADO EGG WRAP *Makes 4*

We love to fill these wraps with avocado and smoked salmon, or avo and turkey – you'll get the perfect dose of protein to get you off to a great start in the morning.

Ingredients
For the wrap
2 eggs
1 garlic clove, crushed
a handful of fresh coriander,
including the stalks, finely chopped
a handful of fresh spinach
2 teaspoons coconut oil, for frying

For the smashed avo
½ avocado
juice of ½ lemon
1 teaspoon paprika
1 garlic clove, crushed

Method
1. In a bowl, mix together the eggs, garlic, coriander and spinach.

2. Put the avocado, lemon juice, paprika and garlic in a separate bowl and mash together with a fork.

3. Melt the oil in a non-stick frying pan over a low heat. Pour about 1 ladleful of the egg mixture into the pan. Rotate the pan so that the mixture spreads out into a thin layer (the thinner the better). Cook for a few minutes until firm and then flip the wrap over to cook the other side. Transfer to a plate and repeat with the remaining batter. The mixture should make about 4 wraps (depending on the size of the frying pan).

4. Spread the smashed avo down the centre of the wrap, roll up and enjoy.

MINI ROASTED VEGETABLE FRITTATAS *Makes 6 mini frittatas*

I love to make these with any leftover roasted veggies from the fridge. Try aubergine, beetroot or roasted broccoli.

Ingredients
2 portobello mushrooms, chopped
1 red pepper, chopped
200g butternut squash, peeled,
deseeded and chopped
2 tablespoons coconut oil, melted
3 asparagus spears, chopped
5 free-range eggs
2 tablespoons unsweetened rice
milk or almond milk
a handful of fresh chives, chopped
a handful of fresh parsley, chopped
1 garlic clove, crushed
sea salt and freshly ground
black pepper
rapeseed oil, for greasing

Method
1. Preheat the oven to 180°C/gas mark 4. Grease a 6-hole muffin tray with rapeseed oil and line it with muffin cases.

2. Put the mushrooms, red pepper and butternut squash on a baking tray and season with salt and pepper. Pour over the melted coconut oil and then bake for about 30 minutes until softened.

3. Meanwhile, put a pan of boiling water over a high heat and blanch the asparagus for a few minutes until cooked but still with a little bite.

4. Beat the eggs and milk together in a bowl. Season well with salt and pepper and mix in the fresh herbs, garlic and asparagus.

5. Once the roasted vegetables are cooked, put a small amount into each muffin case. Divide the egg mixture equally between the muffin cases so that they are three-quarters full. Bake for 18–20 minutes until cooked through. Enjoy warm or store in the fridge and take whenever you need an easy 'breakfast on-the-go'.

GREEN GOODNESS *Serves 2*

Simple, delicious and an oasis of green goodness. Treat your digestive system to a holiday with this abundant alkalising dish. This breakfast has been inspired by our visits to Australia. I think Australia is the world capital of delicious breakfasts.

Ingredients

2 garlic cloves, crushed
4 tenderstem broccoli florets
6 asparagus spears, chopped
3 handfuls of kale, chopped
1 courgette, sliced
juice of ½ lemon
2–4 free-range eggs
½ avocado, chopped
sea salt and freshly ground
black pepper
coconut oil, for frying

Method

1. Heat a frying pan or skillet over a low heat and melt the coconut oil. Add the crushed garlic and cook for about 1 minute.
2. Stir in the broccoli, asparagus, kale and courgette. Squeeze the lemon juice into the pan and season with salt and pepper.
3. Whilst the green goodness is cooking, poach the eggs in a separate pan (use the freshest eggs you can find). Put a pan over a high heat and pour in enough water to come about halfway up the pan. Bring to a simmer and crack the eggs directly into the pan (if you want to be really careful you can crack them into a cup first, one at a time, and then tip them into the water). Poach for about 3–4 minutes until cooked to your liking.
4. Once the eggs are cooked, fill the bowls with the sautéed veg, scatter the avocado over, top with the poached eggs and season with salt and pepper. Feel smug that you've given yourself the best possible start to the day.

AVOCADO AND TURKEY HAM FINGERS *Serves 2*

Ingredients

1 avocado, peeled, stoned and
sliced into long fingers (about
4 per half)
2 tablespoons turmeric powder
a sprinkle of chilli flakes
juice of ½ lemon
a pinch of sea salt
4 slices turkey ham

Method

1. Preheat the grill to medium.
2. Season the avocado with the turmeric, chilli, salt and lemon (but don't go overboard).
3. Wrap two fingers of avocado tightly with a slice of turkey ham and repeat until you have four rolls.
4. Place on a baking tray under the grill and cook on each side for a few minutes or until the avocado starts to get soft and gooey inside.

Top tip!
Always remember
it's great to start the
day off with a dose
of protein.

HOME-BAKED BEANS ON RYE
Serves 2

When you hear baked beans are good for you, this is what they mean – a great vegetarian breakfast that contains a good mix of protein, fat and carbohydrates. Of course if you want to up the protein you can always throw a couple of cooked eggs on top.

Ingredients

1 onion, chopped
2 garlic cloves, crushed
1 x 400g tin cannellini beans
1 x 400g tin chopped tomatoes
1 tablespoon tomato purée
1 tablespoon maple syrup
1 tablespoon tamari sauce
1 tablespoon Worcestershire sauce
1 teaspoon paprika
2 slices rye bread, toasted
sea salt and freshly ground
black pepper
coconut oil, for frying

Method

1. Heat a saucepan over a medium heat and add the coconut oil. Once melted, add the onion and sauté for a few minutes until softened, then add the garlic and stir.

2. Add the beans and chopped tomatoes, followed by the tomato purée, maple syrup, tamari sauce, Worcestershire sauce and paprika. Simmer for 5–10 minutes and season to taste. Serve on slices of toasted rye bread.

TURMERIC AND SPINACH SCRAMBLE
Serves 1

Turmeric is the hippest spice in town. It's used as a powerful anti inflammatory in many cultures and I have witnessed its wonderful healing powers first hand. Use it as much as you can in your cooking.

Ingredients

15g butter
2 free-range eggs
1 teaspoon grated fresh turmeric
1 garlic clove, finely chopped
½ red or green chilli,
finely chopped
70g baby spinach
sea salt and freshly ground
black pepper

Method

1. Melt the butter in a small frying pan.

2. Crack the eggs into a bowl with the turmeric, season to taste and whisk until smooth.

3. Put the chopped garlic and chilli into the pan and fry for 30 seconds, then increase the heat to medium, add the chopped spinach and cook until slightly wilted.

4. Pour the whisked eggs over the vegetables, adding more salt and pepper if needed, and gently stir around in the pan with a wooden spoon until cooked to your liking.

SHAKSHUKA *Serves 2*

Shakshuka is a real crowd pleaser and, what's more, it's so easy to make. When you're having a brunch with friends, serve it straight from the frying pan and enjoy the attention and glory you get for rustling up this impressive dish.

Ingredients

1 onion, diced

2 garlic cloves, crushed

1 teaspoon ground cumin

1 teaspoon mild chilli powder

1 teaspoon paprika

1 tablespoon tomato purée

1 aubergine, sliced widthways

1 red pepper, cut into strips

1 yellow pepper, cut into strips

1 x 400g tin chopped tomatoes

1 tablespoon chopped fresh coriander, plus extra for garnish

1 tablespoon chopped fresh parsley

4 free-range eggs

70g spinach

sea salt and freshly ground black pepper

coconut oil, for frying

Greek yogurt or tahini, to serve (optional)

Method

1. Put a deep, large lidded frying pan or skillet over a high heat and melt the coconut oil. Add the onion and sauté for a few minutes until softened. Add the garlic and stir.

2. After a few minutes, add the spices and tomato purée and stir. Add the aubergine and peppers and leave to soften, stirring every couple of minutes.

3. Add the chopped tomatoes and stir. Mix in the fresh coriander and parsley and continue to cook for 10–15 minutes. Season to taste.

4. Using a big spoon, make 4 small wells in each quarter of the mixture to pour the eggs into. Try to pour them in as quickly as you can so that they all have roughly the same cooking time. Cover the pan with the lid and leave the eggs to cook for roughly 3 minutes (make sure you don't overcook them as the runny yolk is the best bit).

5. Just before the eggs are cooked, scatter the spinach over the top, put the lid back on and leave it to wilt for about 30 seconds. Season with salt and pepper and serve. We love to serve this with a spoonful of Greek yogurt or tahini and a sprinkling of fresh coriander.

LEMON SORREL BAKED EGGS *Serves 1*

Ingredients

2 handfuls of lemon sorrel or spinach

a squeeze of lemon (optional)

1 large free-range egg

a handful of Parmesan cheese

sea salt

oil, for frying

Method

1. Preheat the grill to hot.

2. Heat a little oil in a small frying pan over a low heat and cook the sorrel or spinach until just wilted. If you're not using lemon sorrel, simply add a squeeze of lemon juice.

3. Spoon the wilted vegetables into the bottom of a ramekin and crack the egg on top. Cover with Parmesan and place under the grill until the egg is cooked to your liking, approximately 5 minutes.

Your Breakfast
BAD, BETTER & BEST TABLES

BAD	BETTER	BEST
Sugary breakfast cereal The mix of sugar and salt will leave you feeling sluggish.	**Organic, gluten-free cereal** Some supermarkets are now producing fantastic gluten-free cereals. Make sure you check the sugar content though.	**Super Porridge (page 70)** The nuts and seeds add healthy fats, which boosts the metabolism and keep you feeling fuller for longer.
Waffles and maple syrup This combination of sugar and more sugar will leave you sluggish and hungry well before lunch.	**Gluten-free French toast with honey** Eggs are protein-rich and the lack of gluten may keep you fart-free but it's still high in sugar.	**Protein Pancakes (page 71)** High in protein and fat-burning antioxidants that will keep you full of energy until lunch.
Low-fat yogurt with a coffee A low-fat yogurt is just sugar that has been marketed to appear healthy. Coffee is fine and if you take it with milk make sure you use full-fat organic milk.	**Organic yogurt with coffee and coconut oil** Organic yogurt is better but can still be high in sugar, and dairy might not sit well with you. A mix of coconut oil and coffee will boost your metabolism and give you an energy kick to start your day.	**Coconut yogurt or Greek yogurt with berries and seeds with a Clean and Lean Coffee** The perfect blend of protein, fats, carbohydrates, vitamins and minerals.
Croissant This is another sugar-packed breakfast with very little nutritional value; it will leave you feeling sluggish by lunch.	**Wholemeal bread with peanut butter** This has more fibre than a croissant and the peanut butter provides good fats for energy.	**Gluten-free seeded crackers with almond butter** This is the perfect blend of slow-release energy carbs and fat.
Fruit juice This is packed with sugar and has little nutritional value.	**Homemade fruit smoothie** Full of vitamins but still relatively high in fructose.	**Vegetable and fruit smoothie (cucumber, spinach, berries, almond milk and chia seeds)** Nutrient-dense, alkalising and delicious.

Your breakfast should set you up physically and emotionally for the day ahead so that means absolutely no refined sugar – it's simply not worth it. There are so many better options for you and that beautiful body of yours as you will read below.

BAD	BETTER	BEST
Coffee The typical start to the day for breakfast-haters. However, a measly coffee will soon cause your energy levels to flag and leave you starving by lunchtime.	**Clean and Lean Coffee** (coffee, coconut oil, butter, cinnamon, Bodyism Body Brilliance). Body Brilliance gives you a dose of supergreens, a good amount of protein and is packed with antioxidants.	**Morning Metabolic Mocha (page 236)** This is a perfect smoothie with a great range of nutrients to get your day off to a good start. Having a source of protein alongside this would be even better.
Breakfast fry up of fried bread, breakfast sausage, egg and bacon High levels of saturated fat and salt.	**Scrambled eggs, grilled bacon and sausages** Grilling food helps to reduce the saturated fat content, but sausages are often packed with overly processed ingredients.	**Organic scrambled eggs and sausage with buttered spinach** Eggs are the healthiest source of protein that will fire up your metabolism and the greens will provide vitamins and fibre.
Shop-bought Granola People often think this is a healthy option but most brands are packed with unrefined sugar that will send your blood sugar levels through the roof.	**Sugar-free, wheat-free granola** Luckily, there are good health-focused brands available now. Look at the ingredients and find a granola that uses natural sweeteners and wheat-free grains.	**Homemade granola** Delicious Digestion Boosting Granola and Cacao, Carob and Coconut Granola (page 64) both provide a mix of gluten-free grains, nuts and seeds.
White bagel with low-fat cream cheese Starchy and sugar-loaded.	**Multigrain bagel with full-fat cream cheese** Fibre-rich and more energising.	**Oatcakes with almond butter** The perfect blend of low-GI carbs and healthy fats.
White bread with butter and jam Highly processed and with very little protein.	**Wholegrain bread with almond butter** The combination of healthy fats, protein and fibre makes this a much more nutritious option.	**Clean and Lean Bread (page 197)** This gluten-free bread contains protein, healthy fats, fibre and nutrients.

chapter 5

Lunches

BEETROOT AND WILD FENNEL SOUP *Serves 6–8*

Beetroot is very sweet, full of vitamin C and energy-boosting iron, and it can maintain healthy blood pressure.

Ingredients

500g fresh beetroot, topped and tailed, skin left on
1 small onion, finely diced
1 Bramley apple, finely chopped
1 large fennel bulb or a large handful of wild fennel, finely chopped, fronds reserved
1 garlic clove
500ml chicken or vegetable stock
sea salt and freshly ground black pepper
butter, for frying
cream, to serve

Method

1. Put the beetroot in a saucepan and cover with water. Bring to the boil and cook until tender and the skins easily peel off. This can take from 20 minutes to an hour, depending on the size of the beetroot. Discard the skins and chop the flesh into pieces small enough to fit in your blender.

2. Melt a little butter in a pan over a medium-low heat. Add the onion, apple, fennel and garlic and cook, stirring occasionally, until soft and almost transparent. Add the stock and continue cooking for a few minutes.

3. Put the beetroot and stock mixture into a blender and blend until smooth, or leave it a bit chunkier if you prefer. Season to taste and serve with a dollop of cream and some chopped fennel fronds on top.

NETTLE SOUP *Serves 6–8*

Nettles are healthy and free. If you're up for a trip on the wild side, get your gloves on and go foraging to make this delicious comforting soup. I get that this isn't going to be for everyone but if you're an outdoorsy type or on the run from the law, then enjoy this experience of getting your dinner for free from your environment.

Ingredients

50g butter
1 large onion, finely chopped
1 garlic clove, crushed (use wild garlic if you can forage it)
350g nettle tops, thick and damaged stalks discarded, washed and drained (wear rubber gloves to protect your hands from stings)
1 large potato, cubed
1 large carrot, chopped
1 litre vegetable or chicken stock
3 tablespoons goats' curd
sea salt and freshly ground black pepper
extra virgin olive oil, for drizzling

Method

1. Melt the butter in a large saucepan, add the onion and cook gently for 5–7 minutes, or until softened. Add the garlic, nettles, potato, carrot and stock, bring to a simmer and cook gently for about 15 minutes, or until the potato is soft. Remove from the heat.

2. Using a stick blender, purée the soup and season to taste.

3. Ladle into warmed bowls and float a dollop of goats' curd on top. Swirl in a few drops of extra virgin olive oil while the curd melts.

BUTTERNUT SQUASH AND CHESTNUT SOUP *Serves 10*

This is a perfect winter warmer; it's wonderfully comforting and sustaining and goes on the list of foods that feed your soul.

Ingredients

1.5kg butternut squash, peeled,
deseeded and cut into large chunks
3 tablespoons coconut oil, melted
1 onion, chopped
1 garlic clove, crushed
2 litres chicken or vegetable stock
2 thyme sprigs
2 rosemary sprigs
2 bay leaves
juice of 1 lemon
500g chestnuts, peeled and roasted,
plus a handful for garnish
400g chestnut purée
1 Bramley apple, cored and
chopped
sea salt and freshly ground
black pepper

Method

1. Preheat the oven to 200°C/gas mark 6.

2. Place the butternut squash in a roasting tray and drizzle over about 1 tablespoon of the coconut oil. Transfer to the oven and roast for about 25–30 minutes, until the squash is tender and golden brown. Remove from the oven and set aside.

3. Once the squash is cooked, heat the remaining oil in a large saucepan over a medium heat, add the apple, onion and garlic and fry for 10–15 minutes on a low heat, stirring regularly, until softened.

4. Add the stock to the pan along with the roasted squash, the herbs, lemon juice, chestnuts, chestnut purée and apple. Stir and season well. Bring the mixture to the boil, then turn down the heat and simmer for 15–20 minutes. Set aside to cool.

5. Transfer the mixture to a food-processor and blend until smooth, then return it to the pan and heat until warmed through (if the soup seems too thick add a ladleful of water).

6. Serve garnished with sliced roasted chestnuts.

SPICED CAULIFLOWER AND ALMOND SOUP *Serves 4–6*

Ingredients

1 onion, finely diced
2 garlic cloves
500g cauliflower florets
2 teaspoons curry powder
1 litre almond milk
olive oil, for frying
sea salt and freshly ground
black pepper

Method

1. Heat the oil in a pan over a medium heat and cook the onion and garlic with a pinch of salt until the onions are soft, about 8–10 minutes. Add the cauliflower florets and curry powder and stir for a minute.

2. Pour the almond milk into the pan and cover with the lid. Simmer for 45 minutes. Add more seasoning if needed.

3. Blend the soup in batches in a food-processor. Return it to the pan and heat until warmed through.

4. Serve with a sprinkle of freshly ground black pepper and some Clean and Lean bread.

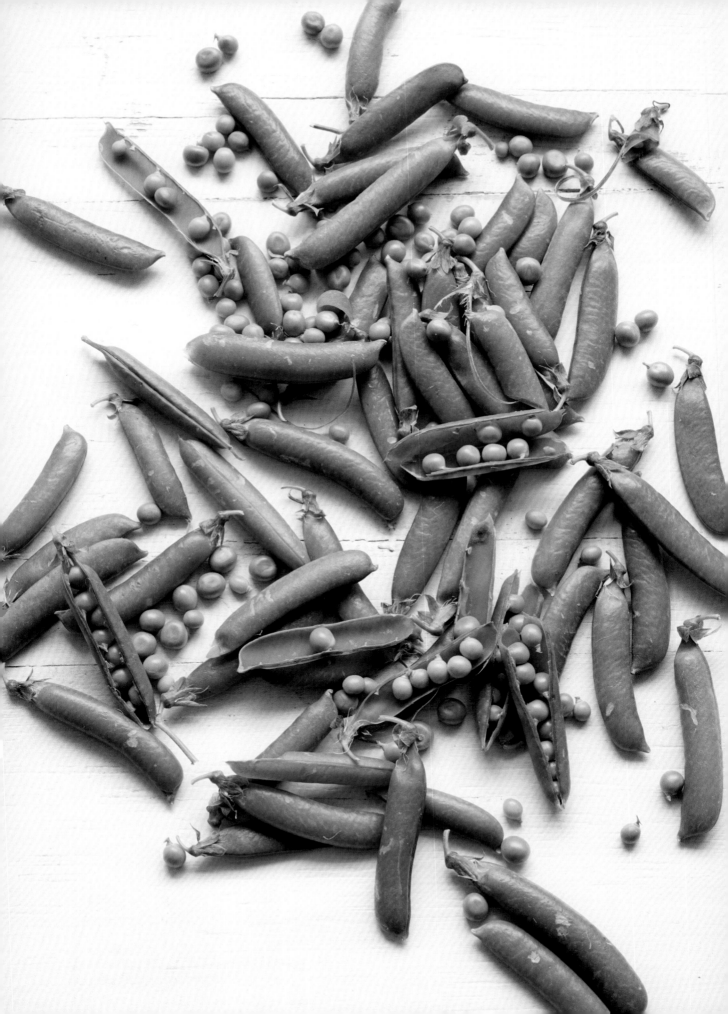

PEA AND LENTIL SOUP *Serves 6–8*

Onions are an underrated vegetable that often get forgotten about, but they're a health powerhouse. They help your body absorb vitamin C more efficiently (which boosts overall health and immunity), they're heart friendly and they help manage blood sugar levels. Even if you think you are a terrible cook, they are a great base to make everything taste good.

Ingredients

1 litre vegetable stock
1 small onion, chopped
2 celery sticks, sliced
1 garlic clove, finely chopped
250g cooked blue or green lentils
250g frozen peas
a handful of parsley
sea salt and freshly ground
black pepper
butter, for frying

Method

1. Heat the stock in a saucepan over a medium heat.

2. Melt a little butter in a small frying pan over a medium heat. Add the onion, celery and garlic with a small pinch of salt. Cook until the vegetables are almost soft, about 5–10 minutes.

3. Once the stock has come to a boil, turn the heat down to low and add the lentils, peas and parsley. Season to taste.

4. Continue to cook for another minute or two and then serve. I try not to cook for too long as everything is already prepared and there is nothing worse than mushy peas in this soup. I like it fresh and still crunchy, but if you prefer you can cook it for longer.

PEA AND MINT SOUP *Serves 4*

This bright and delicious soup is perfect served with a cube of ice in the summer, or warmed up and served with a spoonful of Greek yogurt in the winter. The beauty of it is its simplicity – if I can do it, anyone can.

Ingredients

1 leek, trimmed and sliced
750ml vegetable stock
500g frozen peas
2 handfuls of mint leaves
juice of 1 lemon
sea salt and freshly ground
black pepper
coconut oil, for frying
Greek yogurt, to serve (optional)

Method

1. Melt a little coconut oil in a large saucepan over a medium heat. Add the leek, season and cook until softened, about 8 minutes.

2. Add the stock and peas and continue to cook for 5 minutes. Add the mint and simmer for another 5 minutes. Pour in the lemon juice.

3. Blend until smooth and season well with salt and pepper. Serve warm or cold and add a spoonful of Greek yogurt if you're after something slightly more filling.

SOUP OF ETERNAL YOUTH *Serves 2*

This nourishing alkalising soup is a perfect pick me up if you are feeling a little under the weather. My kids love it as I put little chicken bites in there for them to scoop out – it's a really playful way for them to eat their greens!

Ingredients

2 garlic cloves, finely chopped
½ onion, finely diced
2.5cm piece fresh ginger, peeled
and chopped
1 large broccoli, chopped into
small pieces, including the stalk
150g spinach leaves
3 parsnips, peeled and chopped
2 celery sticks, chopped
a handful of parsley, roughly
chopped
filtered water, as needed (or a
good-quality vegetable stock)
juice of ½ lemon
sea salt and freshly ground
black pepper
olive oil, for frying

Method

1. Heat a little olive oil in a large saucepan over a medium heat. Add the garlic, onion, and ginger and cook for a minute. Add the broccoli, spinach, parsnips, celery and parsley and stir until the spinach wilts.

2. Add just enough water to cover the vegetables. Bring to the boil and then immediately reduce the heat to a simmer and cover the pan. Cook for 10–15 minutes.

3. Use a handheld mixer or food-processor to blend the soup. Season with salt and pepper, stir in the lemon juice and serve.

HEALING BONE BROTH *Serves 10*

Bone broth may sound like something in a witch's cauldron but locked away inside the shell of animal bones is a gigantic amount of essential nutrients and healthy fats, just waiting to nourish your body and soul.

Ingredients

1kg beef or chicken bones (or other
poultry)
4 litres filtered water
3 tablespoons apple cider vinegar
1 onion, roughly chopped
2 carrots, roughly chopped
2 celery stalks, roughly chopped
1 tablespoon peppercorns
1 teaspoon salt
1 bunch of parsley, roughly
chopped
2 garlic cloves, crushed

Method

1. Put the bones in a 5-litre stockpot and add the filtered water. Add the vinegar and leave the bones to sit in the water for 30 minutes. The acidity helps to break down the bones and draw out the calcium.

2. Add the vegetables to the pot with the peppercorns and salt (plus any other spices you may like to add), but reserve the parsley and garlic for now.

3. Bring the broth to a vigorous boil, then reduce to a simmer and simmer until done – 48 hours for beef broth, 24 hours for chicken or poultry broth. For the first 30 minutes you will need to skim and discard scum from the surface. Add the parsley and garlic for the last 30 minutes of cooking.

4. Once cooked, strain through a sieve and store in an airtight container in the fridge for up to 5 days, or freeze for up to 6 months. I like to freeze this in ice cube trays and use a cube when making soups or sauces.

GRAVALAX *Serves 20*

Ingredients

2kg salmon fillet, boned, skin on
160g coconut palm sugar
40g salt
1 teaspoon dill seeds
1 teaspoon freshly ground
black pepper
2 bunches dill, roughly
chopped, stems included

Method

1. Rinse the fish and pat it dry with kitchen paper. Slice the fillet horizontally into 2 equal halves.

2. Pour the sugar and salt into a bowl and combine thoroughly. Pour the mix over the salmon and use your fingers to rub it into the fillets, making sure all the sides are covered. Sprinkle the flesh side of each fillet half with the dill seeds and ground pepper, lightly pressing them into the curing mixture.

3. Place 1 fillet half, flesh-side up, in a dish just large enough to hold it. Place the chopped fresh dill on top of the fillet, then cover it with the second half, flesh-side down. Cover the dish lightly with cling film.

4. Leave the salmon to marinate at room temperature until the sugar/salt mixture has melted into the fillet. This could take up to 6 hours in cold weather, but don't leave it for any longer. You can skip this step entirely in hot weather.

5. Place a small pan or plate on top of the cling film-covered salmon. Weight it lightly with some food tins, for example. Refrigerate for at least 48 hours and up to a week. Every 12 hours, turn the fish over in the brining liquid that has accumulated in the bottom of the dish to ensure that it is evenly marinated all over. Re-cover with the clingfilm and the weighted pan and return to the refrigerator.

6. Remove the cured gravalax from the fridge and scrape off most of the dill and seasonings. Using a sharp knife, cut it into paper-thin slices, pulling each slice away from the skin. Gravalax can be stored in the refrigerator for up to a week and in the freezer for up to a month.

Top tip!
Gravalax is delicious with a wedge of lemon, some sliced beets and a lovely slice of toasted rye.

COURGETTI WITH TOMATOES, GARLIC AND CHILLI *Serves 4*

If you don't have a spiraliser (I talk about these in chapter 3), you can use a vegetable peeler and peel the courgette lengthways into ribbons.

Ingredients

2 teaspoons coconut oil

1 onion, chopped

3 garlic cloves, crushed

1 red or green chilli, deseeded and finely chopped

20 cherry tomatoes, halved

1 tablespoon tomato purée

1 tablespoon tahini

a handful of fresh basil, chopped, reserving a little to garnish

juice of 1 lemon

4 courgettes, spiralised or peeled lengthways into ribbons

a handful of pinenuts, to garnish

sea salt and freshly ground black pepper

Parmesan cheese, grated, to garnish

Method

1. Preheat the oven to 180°C/gas mark 4.

2. Heat a deep frying pan or skillet with 1 teaspoon of the coconut oil. Once melted, add the onion and sauté for a few minutes. Add the garlic and chilli and stir. After a few minutes, add the tomatoes, tomato purée, tahini and basil. Stir well and then add the lemon juice and a ladleful of water. Tip the courgetti into the pan and stir.

3. Meanwhile, put the pine nuts onto a baking tray, spread them out evenly and toast in the oven until golden brown.

4. Once the courgetti is soft, season the mixture and serve into bowls. Scatter the toasted pine nuts over the top and sprinkle with Parmesan and fresh basil.

Top tip!
Plan ahead, make a bit extra for dinner and have it for lunch the next day!

QUINOA TABBOULEH *Serves 4*

Fresh, yummy and with the extra protein coming from the quinoa, this is a great accompaniment to some fresh fish or lean protein or, if you're veggie, sprinkle over the pistachios to make it more filling.

Ingredients

200g quinoa, rinsed
4 beef tomatoes, chopped
1 red onion, chopped
1 cucumber, chopped
1 avocado, chopped
a handful of parsley, chopped
a handful of coriander, chopped
a handful of mint, chopped
juice of 1 lemon
2 tablespoons olive oil
1 tablespoon apple cider vinegar
a handful of pistachios (optional)
sea salt and freshly ground
black pepper

Method

1. Rinse the quinoa well and put it in a saucepan over a medium heat with double the amount of boiling water. Cook for about 10 minutes, until the grain unwraps itself but still has a slight crunch. Drain and rinse well in cold water. Set aside to cool.

2. Tip the cooled quinoa into a salad bowl with all the vegetables and herbs. Drizzle over the lemon juice, olive oil and cider vinegar. Season with salt and pepper and toss to mix it all up.

3. If you want to give your salad an extra crunch, toast the pistachios for a few minutes in the oven and sprinkle them over the top.

WILD GREEN COCONUT AND EGG RICE *Serves 1–2*

You'll notice turmeric is here again. The superhero of spices, it adds great flavour and has wonderful health benefits.

Ingredients

3 free-range eggs
1 chilli, finely chopped
1 garlic clove, finely chopped
3 kale leaves, chopped
a large handful of baby spinach
40g petit pois, defrosted but
not cooked
100g wild rice, cooked
sea salt and freshly ground
black pepper
olive oil, for frying
juice of 1 lemon, to serve
2 tablespoons goats' curd or
natural yogurt, to serve
½ teaspoon grated fresh turmeric
1 teaspoon coconut oil

Method

1. Heat the coconut oil in a small frying pan over a medium heat. Crack the eggs into the pan and scramble them, stirring quickly to break them up. Remove from the pan and set aside.

2. Reduce the heat to low and add a little olive oil to the pan. Add the chilli and garlic and cook for 1 minute. Add the kale, spinach and petit pois and cook for a further minute until wilted, then add the turmeric, cooked rice and egg. Season with salt and freshly ground black pepper.

3. Heat through and serve sprinkled with the lemon juice and topped with the curd.

EASY PEASY CHICKPEA PIZZA *Serves 4*

My kids love it when I say it's pizza time. This healthy version tastes even better than the shop-bought equivalent and is seriously easy to make. We let the kids pick the toppings and love watching them having fun and making a mess in the kitchen with all the fresh vegetables and herbs.

Ingredients
For the base
180g gram flour
1 tablespoon dried oregano
½ teaspoon garlic salt
1 tablespoon dried rosemary
1 tablespoon dried basil
1 teaspoon tamari
1 teaspoon tomato purée
1 tablespoon coconut oil
sea salt and freshly ground black pepper

For the toppings
1 large red pepper, chopped
1 large courgette, sliced
Optional to roast: butternut squash (chopped), aubergine (chopped), red onion (chopped), mushrooms (sliced) and any other veggies leftover in your fridge!
400g organic tinned chopped tomatoes
3 garlic cloves, crushed
1 tablespoon tomato purée
1 teaspoon tamari
1 teaspoon stevia
1 tablespoon red wine vinegar
a handful of rocket
feta cheese (optional)
1 tablespoon, coconut oil, melted

Method:

1. Preheat the oven to 180°C/gas mark 4. Place the pepper, courgette and any other veggies for roasting on a foil-lined baking tray. Drizzle over the melted oil, mix well and place in the oven for about 30 minutes until softened all the way through. Leave to cool.

2. Stir all the base ingredients in a mixing bowl with 230ml water. To make it even easier, blitz the ingredients in a blender (try and get rid of the lumps). Pour the mix into a bowl and leave to stand in the fridge for at least 30 minutes.

3. Heat a saucepan and pour in the tinned tomatoes. Add the garlic, tomato purée, tamari, stevia and red wine vinegar. Stir well and season to taste.

4. Heat a non-stick frying pan with the coconut oil and make sure that the oil lines the whole pan (so that the base will not stick). Once sizzling, pour in a ladleful of batter (so that it is about 25mm thick). Once the base has thickened and can be lifted easily, flip it over and cook the other side until it is golden brown. Place on a foil-lined wire rack and continue frying the mixture until it's all used up.

5. Once all the bases have been placed on the wire rack, spoon on the tomato sauce. Add your toppings and sprinkle with rocket. If you are including cheese (we love to sprinkle feta on the top) add this last.

6. Bake in the oven for 15 minutes. If you have added cheese, grill for the last few minutes so that it goes crispy and golden.

SHREDDED KALE AND MUSHROOM ASIAN SALAD *Serves 4*

Ingredients
For the salad
200g kale, roughly chopped

4 portobello mushrooms, roughly chopped

6 baby sweetcorn, chopped

2 yellow peppers, deseeded and chopped

a handful of cashew nuts

a handful of coconut chips

a handful of coriander, chopped

coconut oil, for grilling

For the dressing
2 tablespoons tamari

2 tablespoons almond butter

1 tablespoon apple cider vinegar

2 teaspoons stevia

juice of 1 lemon

½ red or green chilli, deseeded and chopped

Method
1. Preheat the oven to 180°C/gas mark 4.

2. Chop the kale and mushrooms in a food-processor for a few minutes until shredded into small pieces.

3. Heat a griddle pan and melt a little coconut oil. Cook the baby sweetcorn and peppers until the skins are charred.

4. Put the nuts and coconut on a baking tray and toast in the oven for a few minutes, until golden brown.

5. Put all the ingredients for the dressing in a small bowl with 120ml water and mix well.

6. Put all the salad ingredients into a big salad bowl, toss to combine and dress just before serving.

CHICKPEA, MINT, COURGETTE AND GOATS' CURD SALAD *Serves 2*

Ingredients
2 courgettes, deseeded and peeled into ribbons

1 small red onion or 2 spring onions, chopped

100g peas

1 x 400g tin chickpeas, rinsed and drained

a handful of mint leaves

juice of 1 lemon

a drizzle of extra virgin olive oil

5 tablespoons goats' curd

sea salt and freshly ground black pepper

Method
1. Put all the ingredients except the goats' curd into a salad bowl. Toss to mix and season.

2. Serve topped with the goats' curd.

CRISPY ROSEMARY AND TOMATO SALAD WITH SOURDOUGH CROUTONS *Serves 2*

Rosemary is a great blood cleanser and anti-inflammatory agent. This salad is a healthier way of satisfying a bread craving.

Ingredients

3 tablespoons extra virgin olive oil

2 rosemary sprigs, leaves removed

1 large garlic clove, crushed

2 sourdough bread slices, cubed

1 small cucumber, chopped

250g cherry tomatoes, halved

150g pitted olives

75g feta or labne, crumbled

a splash of apple cider vinegar

sea salt and freshly ground black pepper

Method

1. Heat about 2 tablespoons of the olive oil in a small frying pan over a medium heat. Add the rosemary leaves and fry for about 45 seconds until they crisp up a little, then tip onto kitchen paper to dry.

2. Add the garlic to the pan, followed by the sourdough and season with a little salt. Stir to coat the bread and fry until golden brown, then set aside.

3. Put the cucumber, tomatoes, olives and feta or labne into a small bowl with a splash of apple cider vinegar and the remaining oil. Sprinkle the rosemary over the top and mix.

4. Put the salad into a serving bowl, scatter the garlicky sourdough croûtons on top and serve.

Top tip!
I love adding mint to dishes. It tastes great and aids digestion, so it can ease bloating and other digestive discomforts.

BUCKWHEAT CRÊPES WITH RATATOUILLE *Makes 6 crêpes*

This reminds me of the Marche des Enfants in Paris. Everytime Chrissy and I go, we line up for 45 minutes to get a crepe made by the fabulous Alain who drinks red wine and sings and does everything in his own unique time. It's a special place for Chrissy and so we make this when we are craving a Parisian treat.

Ingredients
For the crêpes
1 onion, chopped
2 garlic cloves, crushed
130g buckwheat flour
1 tablespoon dried oregano
4 free-range eggs
coconut oil, for frying
sea salt and freshly ground
black pepper

For the ratatouille
1 onion, chopped
2 garlic cloves, crushed
1 aubergine, chopped
1 red pepper, chopped
1 yellow pepper, chopped
1 courgette, chopped
1 tablespoon tomato purée
1 tablespoon dried oregano
1 tablespoon dried basil
1 tablespoon apple cider vinegar
1 teaspoon stevia
1 x 400g tin chopped tomatoes
coconut oil, for frying
chopped fresh basil or Parmesan
cheese, to serve (optional)

Method

1. First prepare the crêpe batter. Melt a little coconut oil in a sauté pan over a medium heat. Add the onion and garlic and sauté for about 5 minutes until softened. Set aside to cool.

2. Put the buckwheat flour, cooked onion and garlic and the oregano into a mixing bowl with a little seasoning. Add the eggs and 250ml water and mix well. Leave to rest in the fridge for 15 minutes.

3. While the batter is cooling in the fridge, make the ratatouille. Melt a little coconut oil in a deep saucepan over a medium heat. Add the onion, garlic, aubergine, peppers and courgette. Mix and leave to cook for a few minutes until softened, about 10 minutes. Add the tomato purée, stevia, dried herbs and vinegar, and stir well. Add the chopped tomatoes and season with salt and pepper.

4. Heat the oven to its lowest setting and put a plate in to warm up.

5. To make the crêpes, melt a little oil in a frying pan over a medium heat and swirl it around to cover the base of the pan. Pour a ladleful of batter into the pan and rotate the pan so that the mixture coats the pan in a thin layer. Cook for 1 minute and then flip and cook the other side for 1 minute until the crêpe is lightly browned on both sides. Repeat until the mixture is used up. Place the crêpes on the warm plate, cover them with foil and keep them warm in the oven.

6. To serve, place one crêpe on a serving plate and spread a spoonful of ratatouille on top. Sprinkle with fresh basil or Parmesan, roll up and enjoy!

CHOPPED SALAD *Serves 4*

Ingredients

6 slices cooked turkey breast, diced
4 beef tomatoes, chopped
4 cooked beetroots, chopped
4 cooked artichoke hearts, chopped
1 avocado, chopped
1 cucumber, chopped
1 iceberg lettuce, chopped
1 red onion, chopped
1 x 400g tin sweetcorn, drained
a handful of parsley, chopped

For the dressing

3 tablespoons extra virgin olive oil
1 tablespoon honey
1 tablespoon apple cider vinegar
1 teaspoon Dijon mustard
sea salt and freshly ground
black pepper

Method

1. Put all the salad ingredients into a salad bowl and toss to mix.
2. Put all the ingredients for the dressing in a small bowl, season to taste and stir to mix.
3. Dress the salad and serve. It really is that simple.

Top tip!
This a great packed lunch option for yourself and your children. Just chop and go!

RAINBOW ASIAN SOBA NOODLE SALAD *Serves 4–6*

Ingredients

400g soba noodles
3 peppers (all different colours), deseeded and chopped
½ red cabbage, chopped
8 chestnut mushrooms, sliced
3 spring onions, chopped
1 green eating apple, grated
100g edamame beans
200g beansprouts
a handful of coriander, chopped, to garnish
a handful of coconut flakes, toasted, to garnish

For the dressing

½ red chilli, sliced
5mm-piece ginger, grated
40ml rice wine vinegar
40ml tamari
2 tablespoons almond butter
4 teaspoons stevia
juice of 2 limes
sea salt and freshly ground pepper

Method

1. Cook the noodles according to the instructions on the packet. Tip into cold water to cool.
2. Mix the chopped vegetables, apple, edamame beans and beansprouts together in a salad bowl. Drain the noodles and mix into the rest of the salad.
3. Whisk the dressing ingredients together in a small bowl or food-processor with 120ml water, then season to taste.
4. Toss in the dressing just before serving and sprinkle the coriander and toasted coconut over the top.

RICOTTA PIES WITH COURGETTE CARPACCIO *Serves 4*

As I've said before, if you have an issue with dairy, avoid it. If you don't have an issue with dairy, then enjoy it. If you're not sure if you have an issue with dairy, listen to your body. If you're gassy, bloated or lethargic, it might be your body telling you to avoid it.

Ingredients

600g ricotta
2 tablespoons grated Parmesan cheese
1 heaped tablespoon green or pink preserved peppercorns
a pinch of salt
a small handful of basil leaves
olive oil, for greasing

For the courgette carpaccio

4 courgettes, topped and tailed
1 small red chilli, deseeded and finely chopped
3 tablespoons chopped oregano leaves
2 tablespoons apple cider vinegar
juice and zest of 1 lemon

Method

1. Preheat the oven to 160°C/gas mark 3. Grease 6 small moulds or ramekins.

2. Mix together the ricotta, Parmesan, peppercorns and salt until just combined. Mix in the basil leaves. Spoon into the greased moulds and bake for about 20 minutes, or until golden brown around the edges.

3. While the pies are cooking. Peel the courgettes into long thin ribbons, including the skins but stopping when you get to the seeds (which can be used for something else).

4. Put the courgette ribbons in a serving bowl with all the other carpaccio ingredients. Stir to cover and then chill.

5. Serve the pies with the chilled carpaccio on the side.

> **Top tip!**
> Hallelujah – it's fine to allow cheese into your life, but if you feel bloated it might be an idea to limit the amount you eat.

AVOCADO, BEAN AND MANGO SALSA WITH SPICED PRAWNS *Serves 2*

This recipe is summer on a plate. The vibrant colours of the salad prove that eating well is far from boring.

Ingredients
For the salsa
1 avocado, chopped

½ mango, chopped

100g cannellini beans, drained

½ red onion, diced

1 heritage tomato, chopped

1 teaspoon paprika

1 lemon, squeezed

sea salt and freshly ground black pepper, to season

a handful of coriander (including stalks), chopped to serve

For the prawns
½ teaspoon mild chilli powder

1 teaspoon ground cumin

1 teaspoon ground coriander

1 tablespoon tamari

juice of 1 lemon

150g raw king prawns

1 tablespoon coconut yogurt

Method

1. To make the salsa, add all the ingredients to a bowl and mix. Season well with salt and pepper.

2. To make the prawns, mix the spices, coriander, tamari and lemon in a small bowl, then add the prawns and mix well.

3. On the hob, heat a griddle pan for a few minutes. Add the prawns and leave to cook for a few minutes, until they turn slightly pink.

4. Put the prawns into a small bowl, add the coconut yogurt and mix well. Season with salt and pepper.

5. To serve, spoon the salsa alongside an equal amount of prawns on each plate. Sprinkle with some fresh coriander.

Top tip!
Cannellini beans are a great source of protein, carbs and fibre.

SEA BASS WITH BEETROOT AND FENNEL SLAW *Serves 4*

Ingredients

*3 raw beetroot, peeled and cut
into wedges
2 tablespoons coconut oil, melted
4 small sea bass (about 200g
each), scaled and gutted (ask your
fishmonger to do this)
1 fennel bulb, trimmed and cut
into 5mm slices
2 lemons, sliced
a handful of basil
4 spring onions, chopped
a handful of black olives, pitted
and chopped
50g sesame seeds
2 teaspoons coriander seeds
2 teaspoons cumin seeds
2 teaspoons fennel seeds
a handful of parsley, chopped
a handful of mint, chopped
1 tablespoon sherry vinegar
sea salt and freshly ground
black pepper*

Method

1. Preheat the oven to 200°C/gas mark 6. Line a baking tray with foil.

2. Lay the beetroot on the baking tray with 1 tablespoon of the melted coconut oil. Bake for about 40 minutes, until cooked through.

3. Rinse and dry the sea bass. Stuff the cavity of the fish with some of the fennel slices, lemon and basil and season well with salt and pepper. Place in a roasting dish and scatter with the chopped spring onions, the remaining fennel and the olives. Drizzle with the remaining coconut oil and bake for about 20 minutes until the fish is cooked through and starting to get crispy and brown.

4. Heat a frying pan over a medium heat and toast the sesame, coriander, cumin and fennel seeds. Crush the toasted seeds using a pestle and mortar.

5. In a bowl, mix the roasted beetroot and the cooked fennel from the top of the fish. Add the parsley, mint and the crushed seeds, and then drizzle over the sherry vinegar.

6. Serve the fish with a spoon of slaw on the side.

ASIAN CHICKEN WRAPS *Serves 4*

The chickens don't have to be Asian but the wrap does. The Clean and Lean lettuce wraps have been phenomenally successful, people all over the world have written in their own recipes and take on this brilliant idea. Please feel free to show us your own varieties and instagram them to us @cleanandlean.

Ingredients

4 chicken breasts, cut into small cubes (or salmon or trout fillets)
1 onion, chopped
2 garlic cloves, chopped
1cm cube ginger, grated
4 chestnut mushrooms, chopped
1 iceberg lettuce
a handful of toasted cashews, chopped
a handful of coriander, chopped
coconut oil, for frying

For the marinade

6 tablespoons tamari
1 tablespoon almond butter
1 teaspoon grated fresh ginger
2 garlic cloves, crushed
2 teaspoons stevia

Method

1. Put the ingredients for the marinade in a bowl with 2 tablespoons water and stir well to combine. Add the chicken cubes, cover with cling film and marinate in the fridge for at least 30 minutes.

2. Heat a wok over a low heat for 5 minutes. Melt a little coconut oil, add the onion, garlic, ginger and mushrooms and sauté for about 5 minutes.

3. Meanwhile, separate 8 large leaves from the lettuce and set aside.

4. Tip the chicken mixture into the wok and cook for about 10 minutes, stirring every few minutes, until the chicken is cooked through.

5. Spoon the mixture into the lettuce leaves and sprinkle with the cashews and chopped coriander. Roll up and enjoy!

POTTED SALMON *Serves 4*

Ingredients

400g salmon fillet, skin on
a splash of olive oil
1 heaped tablespoon salted capers
2 tablespoons fennel fronds,
finely chopped
a pinch of salt and white pepper
320g clarified unsalted butter,
cooled (see below)
½ cucumber, to serve
a splash of apple cider vinegar

Method

1. Preheat the oven to 150°C/gas mark 2. Butter 4 ramekins or small dishes.

2. Heat a large, non-stick frying pan over a high heat until hot. Rub the salmon with oil and salt, then place in the hot pan, skin-side down and lower the heat to medium. Cook for a couple of minutes, until the skin is golden brown and crisp at the edges, then turn and cook on the other side for a minute or two until sealed. Add the capers, cover the pan and cook until the salmon is just cooked through. This should only take a couple of minutes, but will depend on the thickness of the fillet.

3. Transfer the salmon to a plate and discard the skin. Use a fork to flake the fish and mash it into a rough paste, discarding any bones.

4. Add a tablespoon of water to the pan and scrape up the pan juices and capers with a wooden spoon, then add them to the salmon along with the fennel, white pepper and a little salt. Use the fork to mix it all together.

5. Divide the salmon mixture between the prepared ramekins and press down to level the surface. Cover with two-thirds of the clarified butter.

6. Transfer the ramekins to a shallow ovenproof dish, add boiling water to come halfway up the sides of the ramekins and cook in the preheated oven for 10 minutes. Remove and leave to cool.

7. Pour the remaining clarified butter over the cooled salmon pots until they are completely covered. Refrigerate for at least 3 hours to set properly.

8. Remove from the fridge 20 minutes before serving to bring back to room temperature. Serve straight from the pots or turn the salmon out onto a plate so that the butter layer is underneath. Just before serving, cut the cucumber into diagonal slices, splash with apple cider vinegar and sprinkle with salt. Serve the potted salmon with the cucumber slices.

Top tip!
If you're dairy sensitive, clarified butter is much easier to digest than regular butter.

COURGETTE, FETA AND GRIDDLED PEACH SALAD *Serves 6*

This is a perfect summer salad. We love to serve this with an Aussie-style barbecue or as a bright delicious starter.

Ingredients

5 courgettes
70g rocket
4 flat bottom peaches, quartered
100g feta, crumbled

For the pesto

300g pumpkin seeds
a generous handful of basil
a generous handful of mint
2 lemons, juice squeezed
120ml water
5 tablespoons olive oil
sea salt and freshly ground
black pepper
a handful of pumpkin seeds,
toasted (for serving)

Method

1. Preheat the oven to 180°C/gas mark 4. Place the pumpkin seeds on a baking tray and season with salt. Place in the oven for about 10 minutes, until the seeds turn golden brown. Once toasted, leave to cool (setting some aside for serving).

2. Use a vegetable peeler to shave the courgette (it is tedious but well worth it). Add the courgette to a salad bowl with the rocket and mix well.

3. In a food processor, add the toasted seeds, basil, mint, lemon juice, water, olive oil and salt and pepper. Blitz together and season with more salt to taste.

4. Pour the pesto over the courgette and rocket and mix really well.

5. Place the peaches in a griddle pan over a high heat and cook until nicely charred, then turn over and cook the other side. Once cooked, leave to cool.

6. Just before serving, add the peaches and feta to the salad bowl and mix really well. Drizzle with an ample amount of olive oil and sprinkle with some reserved pumpkin seeds.

TUNA, BEAN AND HERB SALAD *Serves 1*

Ingredients

1 carrot, chopped into small pieces
1 tomato, chopped
1 small red chilli, finely chopped
½ cucumber, finely chopped
½ red onion, finely chopped
½ red pepper, finely chopped
a handful of basil leaves, torn
a handful of mint leaves, torn
a handful of parsley, torn
1 x 120g tin tuna, drained
½ x 400g tin red kidney beans,
drained and rinsed
25g good-quality hard cheese, such as
Parmesan, cubed
3 tablespoons apple cider vinegar
a good drizzle of extra virgin olive oil
sea salt and freshly ground
black pepper

Method

1. Put all the ingredients in a salad bowl, drizzle with the apple cider vinegar and olive oil, season to taste and serve immediately.

Top tip!
Apple cider vinegar is a wonderful aid for digestion.

ASIAN RED CABBAGE SALAD WITH GLAZED SALMON *Serves 4*

This salmon dish is vibrant and full of colour. Not only will it impress your dinner guests but it also provides the perfect dose of omega-3.

Ingredients

4 salmon fillets
2 garlic cloves, chopped
juice of 2 lemons
a handful of coriander stalks, finely chopped
2 tablespoons tamari
1 teaspoon stevia
20g pecans

For the salad

1 red cabbage, chopped
250g chestnut mushrooms, sliced
300g sugar snap peas, chopped
300g beansprouts
a handful of coriander, chopped

For the dressing

½cm piece of ginger
2 garlic cloves
2 limes
3 tablespoons tamari
2 tablespoons almond butter
3 teaspoons stevia
2 tablespoons water
freshly ground black pepper

Method

1. Preheat the oven to 180°C/gas mark 4. Cut 4 squares of tin foil so that each salmon fillet can be wrapped up into a parcel.

2. Mix the garlic, lemon juice, coriander, tamari and stevia in a bowl, add the salmon fillets and leave to marinade for at least 30 mins.

3. Place each salmon fillet on a square of foil and pour equal amounts of the marinade over each one before wrapping them up.

4. Add all the dressing ingredients to a food processor and blitz well.

5. Mix up all the salad ingredients well in a bowl.

6. Place the salmon in the oven for about 15 minutes. About 5 minutes before taking the salmon out of the oven, place the pecans on a baking tray in the oven and cook until they are toasted. Leave to cool and then chop.

7. Before serving, pour the dressing over the salad and mix well.

8. Serve each fillet on a bed of salad and sprinkle with coriander and pecans.

TOMATO AND BEAN SALAD WITH LEMON-GRILLED MACKEREL *Serves 4*

If the sun is shining, stick the mackerel on the barbecue instead; there is nothing like the smoky taste of fish straight off the grill – it reminds me of being back in Adelaide.

Ingredients
For the salad

400g cannellini beans, drained
250g cherry tomatoes, halved
1 large red onion, thinly sliced
a big handful of basil, chopped,
plus extra to serve
juice of 2 lemons
sea salt and freshly ground
black pepper
2 tablespoons red wine vinegar

For the mackerel

1 tablespoon coconut oil
2 spring onions, chopped
juice of 2 lemons
4 mackerel fillets

Method

1. Mix all the salad ingredients in a bowl and season well.

2. Heat a non-stick frying pan and add the oil. Once sizzling add the spring onions and lemon juice and stir briefly, then fry the mackerel for about 3 minutes on each side.

3. To serve, spoon the salad onto a plate and place the mackerel on top. Sprinkle with some freshly chopped basil leaves and a squeeze of lemon.

CAULIFLOWER STEAKS *Serves 2*

Ingredients

¼ cauliflower, sliced into steaks
6 tablespoons olive oil
1 small red or green chilli,
deseeded and finely chopped
1 teaspoon cumin seeds
1 teaspoon fresh grated or
ground turmeric
1 teaspoon fresh grated or
ground ginger

Method

1. Preheat the oven to 180°C/gas mark 4. Line a baking tray with foil.

2. Season the cauliflower with a tablespoon of the olive oil. Place a small frying pan over a medium heat and fry the cauliflower for 1 minute on each side. Set aside.

3. Mash the spices with the remaining oil in a mortar and pestle, then brush the mixture generously onto each side of the cauliflower and place it on the lined baking tray.

4. Bake for 15 minutes, turning at least once. This is great with the quinoa tabbouleh (see page 104) – a lovely vegetarian option.

Top tip!
Cauliflowers are fantastically versatile and can be sliced into 'steaks' or grated into 'rice'.

Your Lunch
BAD, BETTER & BEST TABLES

BAD	BETTER	BEST
Chicken nuggets and chips Fried foods are loaded with unhealthy trans-fats.	**Chicken burger (no bun) with sweet potato fries** Removing the batter and bun reduces the amount of harmful fats and refined white flour.	**Chicken nuggets (see page 161) with salad** Our healthy take on chicken nuggets is nutrient-dense and low in starchy carbs.
Microwave pasta bake Contains loads of processed ingredients. In my opinion this is the nutritional equivalent of punching yourself in the face.	**Brown rice pasta salad** Brown rice has more fibre than the white pasta equivalent, which is great for digestion	**Quinoa Tabbouleh (see page 104)** A protein-rich lunch with a good dose of colourful vegetables that also happens to be delicious.
Shop-bought filled baguette Full of unhealthy fats, sugar and salt.	**Sourdough sandwich with chicken or turkey and vegetables** Less-refined carbs and protein will keep you fuller for longer	**Chicken or turkey salad with vegetables** Choose fillings like chicken, turkey and tuna and serve with a good portion of delicious salad
Jacket potato with cheese, baked beans and coleslaw The jacket itself isn't bad, it's the fillings. Tinned beans and premade coleslaw are often filled with sugar and other processed ingredients.	**Jacket poato with tuna and soured cream** Soured cream is a better option than the long-life grated cheese that is often served at a jacket potato counter and tuna will give you a protein boost.	**Sweet potato, butter, tuna and smashed avocado** The avocado gives you a great source of good fats and will taste delicious with tuna too.
Instant soup This highly processed powdered version of a soup is empty of any nutritional value.	**Fresh supermarket soups** Many of these are full of healthy vegetables. Just try and opt for varieties that are not laden with cream and low-quality oils.	**Pea and Mint Soup (see page 99)** Fresh ingredients and homemade stock give you a dose of wonderful vitamins and minerals.

A lot of us are so busy during the week that lunch becomes an afterthought. Suddenly, hunger strikes and we rush out and grab the quickest thing we can find – a pre-prepared sandwich or a salad full of additives and little goodness. However, there are easy, healthy and delicious alternatives, see below.

BAD	BETTER	BEST
Cheese toastie I would not call processed cheese slices real food. When toasted on white bread too, this is a high-calorie, low-quality meal.	**Organic cheese on sourdough** Opt for organic dairy products and your tummy will definitely thank you for it.	**Organic high-quality cheese with Clean and Lean Bread (see page 197)** Our delicious recipe is packed with wonderful nutrients. Simply serve with some organic butter and a slice of organic cheese.
Crisps, shop-bought salad and a banana Shop-bought salads aren't as healthy as you might assume, the dressings are often packed with low-quality ingredients.	**Root vegetable crisps, shop-bought salad with homemade dressing, and a banana** Keep olive oil and a lemon on your desk at work to dress your salad with and buy vegetable crisps as they contain more nutrients.	**Home-baked Kale Crisps (see page 176), homemade fresh salad and a banana** Making your own crisps means they will be unprocessed and more delicious. A homemade salad will be much tastier too.
White rice sushi Can irritate your digestive system, leaving you bloated and lethargic.	**Brown rice sushi** Brown rice provides a great source of magnesium, which helps you sleep better.	**Quinoa sushi with seaweed salad** A great dose of protein and the seaweed salad will give you a tasty portion of greens. This is much better for you than any other equivalent.
Cheese and beans on toast Highly processed pre-sliced cheese is not good for you – it's a real irritant for our digestive system.	**Grass-fed cheese and beans on wholemeal toast** Grass-fed cheese will save your digestive system a lot of stress. Wholemeal bread contains many more nutrients than white bread.	**Homemade Baked Beans on Rye Bread (see page 87) with organic, grass-fed cheese** Homemade baked beans are packed with fibre and are free from sugar and high levels of salt.

chapter 6

Dinners

GREEN GNOCCHI *Serves 2–4*

Ingredients

100g broad beans, shelled

200g spring greens, washed

a handful of parsley,
finely chopped

1 garlic clove, crushed

140g ricotta

85g buckwheat flour, plus extra
for dusting

2 free-range eggs

100g Parmesan cheese, grated,
plus extra to serve

½ teaspoon freshly grated nutmeg

100g butter

a handful of wild garlic, finely
chopped, or use 2 garlic cloves

sea salt and freshly ground
black pepper

Method

1. Line a baking tray with baking paper.

2. Put the shelled broad beans in a pan over a high heat and just cover with boiling water. Boil for 3–4 minutes. Remove and set aside.

3. Place the greens in a large bowl and pour boiling water over them. Leave for 1–2 minutes until wilted, drain thoroughly and then finely chop.

4. Place the greens, parsley, garlic, ricotta, flour, eggs, Parmesan and nutmeg into a large bowl and season with salt and pepper. Use a fork to stir very thoroughly until everything is completely mixed.

5. Tip the mixture onto a lightly floured surface and gather into a ball. Take a portion of the dough and roll it into a finger-sized sausage shape, then cut it into 3cm portions. Repeat with the rest of the dough.

6. Place the gnocchi on the lined baking tray and refrigerate for at least 30 minutes.

7. Put the butter in a frying pan over a low heat with the chopped wild garlic or finely chopped garlic. Leave to melt while you cook the gnocchi.

8. Bring a pan of water to the boil. Lower the gnocchi into the water in batches using a slotted spoon. When they rise to the surface, after about 2–3 minutes, they're cooked. Remove from the pan and keep warm while you cook the rest of the gnocchi. Serve hot.

9. Pour the melted wild garlic butter over the cooked gnocchi and toss so that they're all covered in the butter. Serve with a sprinkling of Parmesan.

Top tip!
It's better to use a little strong-flavoured Parmesan rather than lots of cheaper, milder-tasting processed cheese.

SPICY STUFFED MARROW *Serves 2*

Marrow and squash are such filling, delicious vegetables. Depending on the season, I like to experiment with different varieties. This is such an easy dish to make, yet the strong flavours make it seriously tasty.

Ingredients

1 large marrow, halved lengthways and deseeded (if you can't find a marrow, use a squash)
½ onion, finely diced
1 carrot, finely chopped
½ large fennel bulb, finely diced
1 garlic clove, crushed
1 small red or green chilli, finely chopped
1.5cm piece of fresh turmeric, grated
100g cooked quinoa
a handful of parsley, finely chopped
a pinch of cayenne pepper
1 lemon, halved
20g Parmesan cheese, grated
30g goats' curd
sea salt and freshly ground black pepper
olive oil, for drizzling and frying

Method

1. Preheat the oven to 180°C/gas mark 4. Line a baking tray with foil.

2. Lay the marrow halves on the lined baking tray, skin-side up, and drizzle them with olive oil. Put them in the oven to start cooking while you make the stuffing.

3. Heat a little oil in a frying pan over a medium heat and cook the onion for a few minutes until soft. Add the carrot, fennel, garlic, chilli and turmeric and cook for another couple of minutes. Add the cooked quinoa, parsley and cayenne pepper and season to taste. Remove from the heat.

4. Remove the baking tray from the oven and turn the marrow halves over so that they're skin-side down. Carefully stuff the marrow with the quinoa stuffing, sprinkle with the grated Parmesan and cook for another 5–10 minutes or until the marrow is soft. Squeeze one lemon half over the marrows and slice the other half in half again.

5. Serve topped with the goats' curd and the lemon quarters on the side.

Top tip!
I'm always so thankful that I'm fortunate enough to be eating something at the end of my day. Make it a special time.

SEXY PESTO *Serves 4*

Pumpkin seeds provide the perfect protein boost and, even more exciting, it is an aphrodisiac! This pesto is filled with a range of other sexy ingredients including parsley, basil and garlic. Whip this up and serve with wholegrain pasta or spread over salmon for a special Valentine's meal.

Ingredients

60g pumpkin seeds, toasted
1 garlic clove, crushed
juice of 1 lemon
a handful of basil
½ handful of parsley
1 teaspoon apple cider vinegar
4 tablespoons olive oil
120ml water
sea salt and freshly ground
black pepper

Method

1. In a food processor, blitz the toasted pumpkin seeds, garlic, lemon, basil, parsley and vinegar.

2. Once a paste has formed, add the oil and blitz again. Add enough water until it looks like the perfect sauce substance. Season with salt and pepper.

3. Store in a mason jar and keep in the fridge to spoon on quinoa or oatcakes whenever you are after a saucy, tasty aphrodisiac! We love to sprinkle the sauce with Parmesan. The pesto can be frozen for up to 3 months.

COURGETTI WITH KALE PESTO *Serves 2*

Add some grilled salmon or aubergine to make this a more hearty dinner.

Ingredients

4 courgettes, spiralised or peeled
into ribbons to the seed
a large handful of parsley
a large handful of mint
6 kale leaves
1 small red or green chilli,
deseeded and chopped
1–2 garlic cloves, peeled
juice of 1 lemon
100g Parmesan cheese, grated
2 tablespoons extra virgin olive oil
40g pine nuts, toasted
sea salt and freshly ground
black pepper

Method

1. Start by making the pesto. Put the herbs, kale, chilli and garlic into a food processor and blitz until fine. Add the lemon juice, Parmesan and salt to taste. Add the olive oil slowly until the pesto is the right consistency. Add more oil if it is too dry.

2. Place a small saucepan of water over a high heat and bring to the boil. Blanche the courgette ribbons for 30 seconds, strain and place back into the dry saucepan.

3. Add the pesto and stir over the heat until mixed through. Sprinkle the pine nuts on top and serve.

BEJEWELLED AUBERGINE *Serves 6*

Ingredients

3 aubergines, halved lengthways
1 teaspoon coconut oil, melted
10 tablespoons Greek yogurt
2 tablespoons lemon juice
1 tablespoon za'atar
1 tablespoon tahini
3 tablespoons flaked almonds
3 tablespoons pomegranate seeds
a handful of parsley, chopped
sea salt and freshly ground
black pepper
olive oil, for drizzling

Method

1. Preheat the oven to 180°C/gas mark 4.

2. Prick the aubergine halves with a fork and place them skin-side down on a baking tray. Drizzle with the melted coconut oil, season with salt and pepper and bake for 20 minutes, until the flesh is soft.

3. Meanwhile, mix the yogurt with the lemon juice, za'atar, tahini and a pinch of salt and pepper.

4. Once the aubergines are cooked, remove them from the oven and set aside to cool slightly. Scatter the almonds over a clean baking tray in an even layer and toast them for a few minutes in the hot oven, until golden brown.

5. Place the aubergines on a large platter. Spoon the yogurt mixture over the top and sprinkle with the toasted almonds, pomegranate seeds and parsley. Drizzle with olive oil and season with salt and pepper.

TURKEY AND QUINOA MEATLOAF *Serves 2*

Ingredients

250g turkey mince
125g cooked quinoa
2 carrots, grated
1 beetroot, grated
1 courgette, grated
1 shallot, finely sliced
zest and juice of ½ lemon
2 tablespoons grated Parmesan cheese
1 teaspoon grated fresh turmeric
a drizzle of olive oil
sea salt and freshly ground
black pepper
butter or oil, for frying

Method

1. Preheat the oven to 180°C/gas mark 4. Grease a 450g loaf tin with butter or oil.

2. Put all the ingredients in a medium-sized bowl and mix thoroughly, then transfer to the tin and press down firmly. Brush with a little more oil.

3. Bake for 25–30 minutes or until cooked through.

Top tip!
Aubergines are full of antioxidants. Their spongy texture also means they absorb herbs and spices easily so are wonderful to cook with.

CHICKEN AND LEEK QUINOA RISOTTO *Serves 4*

This makes a delicious, hearty lunch or dinner. If you are vegetarian, just swap the chicken with some lovely fresh chunky mushrooms.

Ingredients

2 teaspoons coconut oil
1 onion, chopped
3 garlic cloves, chopped
2 celery sticks, chopped
6 asparagus spears, chopped
1 leek, chopped
170g quinoa, rinsed
1 tablespoon balsamic vinegar
1½ litres home-made chicken broth
(or very good-quality bought stock)
100g peas
zest and juice of 1 lemon
a few sprigs of oregano or
rosemary, leaves separated
75g grated Parmesan cheese
2 cooked chicken breasts, chopped
sea salt and freshly ground
black pepper
a handful of rocket, to serve
olive oil, for dressing

Method

1. Heat the coconut oil in a deep skillet or frying pan over a medium heat. Add the onion and sauté until softened, then add the garlic, celery, asparagus and leek and leave to sauté for a further 10 minutes.

2. Add the rinsed quinoa and stir until it is well coated by the mixture. Add the balsamic vinegar and stir well.

3. Add the stock, a ladleful at a time, waiting for the quinoa to absorb the liquid each time. After about 10 minutes the quinoa should be almost cooked. Add the peas, lemon zest and juice, herbs and Parmesan. Mix in the chicken, stir well and season to taste.

4. To serve, sprinkle over the rocket and some more Parmesan and drizzle with olive oil.

WILD MUSHROOM, FENNEL, QUINOA AND GOATS' CURD *Serves 1*

Ingredients

20g butter
1 garlic clove, crushed
6 large wild mushrooms, sliced
100g cooked quinoa
2 oregano sprigs, chopped
a handful of fennel fronds
20g Parmesan cheese
1 tablespoon apple cider vinegar
a drizzle of olive oil
sea salt and freshly ground
black pepper

Method

1. Melt the butter in a medium frying pan. Add the garlic and mushrooms and a tiny bit of salt. As soon as they start to soften, add the cooked quinoa and stir. Add the oregano, Parmesan and fennel fronds and cook for a further minute.

2. Remove from the heat and add the vinegar and a drizzle of oil. Season to taste.

PRAWN AND CASHEW ASIAN STIR-FRY *Serves 4*

The key to a stir-fry is keeping things crunchy and so always cook your vegetables for a little less time than you think. Red cabbage is a fantastic addition to salads and stir-fries as it adds colour, flavour, texture and crunch.

Ingredients

1 tablespoon sesame oil

1 onion, chopped

2 garlic cloves, chopped

½ red or green chilli, deseeded and chopped

2 red peppers, chopped

2 courgettes, chopped or spiralised

8 Tenderstem broccoli spears

½ red cabbage, chopped

3 tablespoons tamari sauce

1 teaspoon stevia (if you need to add a little bit of sweetness)

1 tablespoon tahini

juice of 1 lemon

1 tablespoon almond butter

a handful of cashews

a handful of coconut chips

20 raw king prawns, shelled and deveined

Method

1. Preheat the oven to 180°C/gas mark 4.

2. Heat the sesame oil in a large wok over a high heat. Add the onions, garlic, chilli, red peppers, courgettes, broccoli and red cabbage, followed by the tamari, stevia, tahini, lemon and almond butter. Stir well.

3. Put the cashews and coconut chips on a baking tray and toast in the oven for a few minutes until golden brown. Remove from the oven.

4. Add the prawns to the wok and cook for a few minutes until the prawns turn a pale orange colour and are cooked through. Serve with a sprinkling of the toasted cashews and coconut chips.

Top tip!
Prawns are a great source of protein and soak up flavours from other ingredients really well, making them perfect for spicy dishes.

COCONUT LENTIL CURRY *Serves 4–6*

For me, this is pure comfort food. I love this in a big bowl, with a spoon of coconut yogurt.

Ingredients

1 medium-sized butternut squash,
peeled and diced

2 carrots, chopped

4 garlic cloves, finely chopped

7.5cm piece fresh ginger, grated

2 onions, finely chopped

1 x 400g tin coconut cream

1 litre good-quality vegetable stock
or bone broth (see page 100)

250g puy lentils

500ml boiling water

1 chilli, finely chopped

5cm piece fresh turmeric, grated

½ teaspoon cayenne pepper

juice of 1 lemon

small bunch of coriander, chopped

sea salt and freshly ground
black pepper

Method

1. Put the squash, carrot, garlic, ginger, onions, coconut cream and stock in a pan over a low heat, put the lid on and bring to a simmer. Cook for about 15 minutes.

2. Add the lentils, boiling water and the rest of the spices. Season and continue to cook for 20 minutes, tasting often and adjusting the seasoning to taste as needed.

3. Remove from the heat, add the lemon juice and coriander and serve.

JAMES' MUM'S CHICKEN CURRY *Serves 4*

This curry will go down in the Duigan family tree – it is my favourite meal from my childhood and is quickly becoming Charlotte's favourite too. It's really simple to make and yet so full of goodness and flavour.

Ingredients

½ onion, chopped

10 cardamom pods

10 cloves

5mm-piece fresh ginger, grated

2 cinnamon sticks

500g boneless and skinless chicken
thigh, diced

1 teaspoon ground turmeric

2 teaspoons tomato purée

1 x 160ml tin coconut cream

sea salt and freshly ground
black pepper

brown rice or quinoa, to serve

Method

1. In a deep saucepan over a medium heat, soften the onion in a little water, then add the cardamom, cloves, ginger and cinnamon sticks. Stir and leave to simmer for 5 minutes.

2. Add the chicken and stir, then add the turmeric and tomato purée and mix again. Leave to cook for about 20 minutes. If it seems dry, add a ladleful of water.

3. Once the chicken is cooked through, add the coconut cream and season well with salt and pepper.

4. Serve on a bed of brown rice or quinoa.

MIDDLE EASTERN-STYLE TROUT WITH CAULIFLOWER RICE *Serves 2*

Cauliflower rice is great when you are looking to limit your starchy carbs. The great thing about it is that it actually tastes delicious too.

Ingredients
For the trout
2 trout fillets
juice of 1 lemon
1 tablespoon za'atar
a handful of mint, chopped, plus
2 sprigs to garnish

For the cauliflower rice
½ cauliflower, florets removed and stalk discarded
½ onion, chopped
1 garlic clove, chopped
¼ red or green chilli, deseeded and chopped
3 tablespoons tamari
3 tablespoons tahini
zest and juice of 1 lemon
1 teaspoon ground cumin
1 teaspoon turmeric powder
coconut oil, for frying

Method

1. Preheat the oven to 180°C/gas mark 4. Line a baking tray with foil and place another tray in the oven to heat up. Cut 2 squares of foil large enough to wrap the trout fillets, leaving a little bit of air inside.

2. Place each trout fillet in the centre of a foil square. Sprinkle with half the lemon juice, the za'atar and the chopped mint. Bring the sides of the foil squares up over the fish and fold to close. Fold the foil ends over to make sealed pockets for the fish to steam inside. (Don't wrap the fish tightly; you want to leave a little air inside.) Chill in the fridge until you're ready to start cooking.

3. Meanwhile, make the cauliflower rice. Put the cauliflower florets into a food processor and whizz to the consistency of rice.

4. Melt a little coconut oil in a large frying pan or skillet over a low heat. Add the onion, garlic and chilli and leave to sauté for about 6–7 minutes.

5. Place the fish fillets on the hot baking tray and steam in the oven in their foil pockets for 15 minutes.

6. While the fish is cooking, pour the cauliflower rice into the frying pan and stir. Add the tamari, tahini, the lemon juice and zest, and the spices and cook on a low heat for 5 minutes. Once cooked, cover with a lid and turn off the heat.

7. Serve the fish on a bed of cauliflower rice, garnished with a sprig of mint and some fresh greens on the side.

KALE-STUFFED BAKED TROUT *Serves 4–6*

Ingredients

5 kale leaves

a large bunch of parsley, finely chopped

1 small red chilli, deseeded and finely chopped

4 tablespoons olive oil

4 tablespoons apple cider vinegar, plus extra to drizzle

2 lemons

1 whole trout, about 1kg, scaled and gutted (ask your fishmonger to do this for you)

sea salt and freshly ground black pepper

Method

1. Preheat the oven to about 180°C/gas mark 4.

2. Put the kale, parsley, chilli, olive oil, vinegar and the juice and zest of 1 of the lemons into a small bowl. Season and mix it all together. Slice the other lemon into rounds.

3. Place the fish in the centre of a large sheet of foil big enough to wrap it in. Lay half the lemon slices inside the cavity of the fish. Spoon the kale stuffing evenly over the lemon slices.

4. Season the skin of the fish with salt and pepper and a drizzle of oil, rubbing the seasoning into the skin with your fingers.

5. Place the remaining lemon slices along the length of the fish and hold them in place with toothpicks.

6. Wrap the sides of the foil over the fish and fold to close. Fold up the ends and seal to create a pocket for the fish to steam inside. Don't wrap the fish tightly; you want to leave a little air inside.

7. Bake for about 30 minutes or until the flesh is just cooked and falling off the bone.

Top tip!
For the cleanest fish and best flavour, always try to buy local and in season.

ASIAN SALMON BITES WITH AVOCADO DIP *Serves 4*

This is fresh soul food for healthy people. It is a light yet satisfying dinner option and the wasabi dip will certainly get your taste buds attention.

Ingredients
For the dumplings

1 white onion

2 garlic cloves

0.5cm piece of fresh ginger

½ red or green chilli, deseeded

4 salmon fillets, cut into chunks

a handful of coriander

1 tablespoon tamari

1 teaspoon fish sauce

juice of 1 lime

sea salt and freshly ground black pepper

coconut oil, for frying

cooked brown rice or quinoa, to serve (optional)

For the avocado wasabi dip

2 avocados

1 garlic clove, finely chopped

juice of 1 lime

1 tablespoon tamari sauce

1 tablespoon wasabi paste

chopped fresh coriander leaves, to serve (optional)

Method

1. Put the onion, garlic, ginger and chilli into a food processor and whizz. Add the salmon chunks, coriander, tamari, fish sauce and lime juice. Blitz until the mixture has a mincemeat-like consistency (not for too long or it will become too smooth).

2. Tip the mixture into a bowl and season lightly. Wet your hands and then take a spoonful of the mixture and roll it in your palms into a ball. Repeat until the mixture is used up, then chill the balls in the fridge for 10 minutes.

3. Heat a frying pan over a medium heat and melt a little oil. Sear the dumplings in the pan for about 1–2 minutes on each side, then remove from the pan and set aside.

4. Prepare a steamer. Add the dumplings and steam to cook through for about 10 minutes.

5. Meanwhile, make the avocado dip. Halve and stone the avocados, scoop out the flesh and mash it with a fork. Add the rest of the ingredients and mix thoroughly. Garnish with coriander, if using, just before serving.

6. These dumplings are delicious served alongside some brown rice or quinoa with a spoonful of the avocado wasabi dip.

Top tip!
Avocados are full of healthy fats. They also contain beta carotene which is great for eye-sight, cell growth and fertility.

HERBY POACHED FISH *Serves 2*

Ingredients

2 shallots, finely chopped
750ml chicken or vegetable stock
zest and juice of 3 lemons
a bunch of basil leaves
a bunch of lemon thyme
a bunch of parsley sprigs
3 garlic cloves, smashed
½ teaspoon peppercorns
2 in season white fish fillets,
such as cod or plaice
sea salt and freshly ground
black pepper
olive oil, for frying
wilted fresh seasonal greens,
to serve

Method

1. Heat a little oil in a pan over a low heat. Add the shallots and cook until soft, about 3–4 minutes. Stir in the stock, lemon juice and zest, herbs, garlic and peppercorns. Bring the mixture to a simmer.

2. While the liquid heats up, season both sides of the fish fillets with salt and pepper.

3. Reduce the heat to low and add the fish to the pot. Cover and cook for 8–10 minutes, or until the fish is opaque and flaky.

4. Remove the fish from the pan. Strain the poaching liquid, discarding the solids, and serve the fish in the liquid with some fresh seasonal greens.

BAKED COD, TOMATO AND AUBERGINE *Serves 2*

Ingredients

85g quinoa
600g tinned chopped tomatoes
2 garlic cloves, crushed
1 onion, chopped
1 aubergine, chopped
1 red pepper, deseeded and chopped
1 tablespoon dried oregano
1 tablespoon red wine vinegar
1 teaspoon stevia
a handful of basil, chopped
2 cod fillets, chopped into chunks
a handful of hazelnuts, chopped
a handful of pine nuts
sea salt and freshly ground
black pepper

Method

1. Preheat the oven to 180°C/gas mark 4. Line a baking tray with baking paper.

2. Bring 240ml water to the boil in a saucepan over a medium heat. Add the quinoa and season with salt and pepper. Cook for about 15 minutes, until you can see the curlicue in each grain. Drain away any excess water.

3. Tip the cooked quinoa onto the lined baking tray and spread it out evenly. Bake for about 30 minutes, until crispy and golden brown.

4. Heat the chopped tomatoes in a deep frying pan. Add the garlic and onions and stir well. After 10 minutes, add the aubergine and pepper and stir well. Add the oregano, red wine vinegar, stevia and basil and leave to cook for at least 20 minutes, stirring occasionally. Take off the heat.

5. Add the cod chunks to the tomato sauce, pour into a casserole dish and bake for about 15 minutes. Remove from the oven. Spoon the baked quinoa over the top and sprinkle with the chopped nuts and pine nuts. Season with salt and pepper and return to the oven for another 10 minutes. Serve straight away.

SWEET POTATO FISH PIE *Serves 4–6*

There is something about fish pie that makes me think about winter and cosy nights in. If you love cheese and have no problem with it, sprinkle it over the top of the pie so it melts into the mash in the oven.

Ingredients

500g sweet potatoes, peeled and cut
into 2cm chunks
½ onion, finely diced
1 carrot, peeled and cubed
2 celery sticks, thinly sliced
½ red or green chilli, deseeded and
very finely chopped
125g frozen peas
100g good-quality melting cheese,
such as Cheddar, grated (optional)
zest and juice of 1 lemon
4 flat-leaf parsley sprigs,
finely chopped
300g salmon fillets, skinned, boned
and cut into bite-sized chunks
300g in season white fish fillets,
such as haddock or cod, skinned,
boned and cut into bite-sized
chunks
125g raw prawns, peeled
60ml double cream, plus extra
to drizzle
2 large knobs of butter
olive oil
sea salt and freshly ground
black pepper

Method

1. Preheat the oven to 200°C/gas mark 6.

2. Put the sweet potato chunks in a large pan of cold salted water and bring to the boil. Cook for about 12 minutes, until soft enough to mash.

3. Put the onion, carrot, celery, chilli and frozen peas into a 1.5 litre baking dish. Scatter the lemon zest and the parsley over the top. Now add the fish pieces and the prawns, the lemon juice and the cream. Drizzle with olive oil and season with a good pinch of salt and pepper. Mix everything together.

4. Drain your cooked potatoes in a colander, then return them to the pan, add the butter, a pinch of salt, lots of pepper and a drizzle of cream. Mash with a stick blender or potato masher and spread evenly over the top of the pie filling. Top with the grated cheese, if using.

5. Bake for about 40 minutes, or until cooked through, crispy and golden on top.

Top tip!
Chilli contains more vitamin C than oranges and can help improve digestion and clear sinus congestion.

PRAWN AND COCONUT CURRY *Serves 4*

Ingredients

1 onion, chopped
2 garlic cloves, crushed
½ red or green chilli, deseeded
and chopped
1 teaspoon ground turmeric
1 teaspoon ground cinnamon
1 teaspoon mild chilli powder
1 teaspoon ground cumin
1 tablespoon tomato purée
1 teaspoon garam masala
2 aubergines, sliced widthways
250g butternut squash, chopped
1 x 400g tin coconut milk
1 x 400g tin chopped tomatoes
1 x 400g tin chickpeas, drained
400g raw tiger prawns, peeled
a handful of cashew nuts (optional)
a handful of coconut flakes
(optional)
2 handfuls of spinach
a handful of coriander leaves,
chopped
coconut oil, for frying
cooked quinoa or wholegrain rice,
to serve (optional)

For the raita

6 tablespoons Greek yogurt
½ cucumber, finely chopped
a handful of mint, finely chopped
1 garlic clove, crushed
sea salt and freshly ground
black pepper

Method

1. If you are using cashew nuts and coconut flakes, preheat the oven to 180°C/gas mark 4.

2. Melt a little oil in a large saucepan over a medium heat and sauté the onion and garlic for a few minutes. Add the chilli, turmeric, cinnamon, chilli powder, cumin, tomato purée and garam masala and stir. Add the aubergine slices and squash and mix well.

3. Pour in the coconut milk and chopped tomatoes and leave to simmer for 20 minutes, stirring every few minutes. Once the squash begins to soften, add the chickpeas and stir. Place the lid on the saucepan and leave to simmer away until the squash is cooked through.

4. Mix all the ingredients for the raita together in a bowl and season with salt and pepper.

5. Add the prawns to the curry and stir well. Leave to cook for about 5 minutes, until the prawns are cooked through. The curry should have a stew-like consistency. If needed, add a ladle of water and mix through.

6. Toast the cashews and coconut, if using, in the oven for a few minutes, until golden brown, then season well with salt and pepper.

7. Just before serving, throw the spinach into the curry and leave to wilt for a couple of minutes.

8. Serve the curry with a sprinkling of toasted cashews and coconut and some fresh coriander, with a spoonful of raita on top. This curry is best served on a bed of quinoa or wholegrain brown rice.

Top tip!
Turmeric, an antioxidant powerhouse, has been an integral element of Indian medicine for centuries.

TURKEY MEATBALLS WITH COURGETTI *Serves 4*

Ingredients

500g lean turkey mince
2 onions, chopped
3 garlic cloves, crushed
1 red pepper, deseeded and chopped
a handful of basil
2 tablespoons dried oregano
1 tablespoon dried rosemary
2 free-range eggs, lightly beaten
2 tablespoons tomato purée
2 portobello mushrooms, chopped
1 leek, chopped
2 x 400g tins chopped tomatoes
1 tablespoon apple cider vinegar
3 courgettes, spiralised
sea salt and freshly ground
black pepper
coconut oil, for frying
Parmesan cheese, grated, to serve

Method

1. Preheat the oven to 180°C/gas mark 4.

2. Put the turkey, onion, 2 of the crushed garlic cloves, the red pepper, basil, half the oregano, the rosemary, and some salt and pepper into a bowl and mix well. Stir in the eggs and half the tomato purée.

3. Wet your hands and roll a spoonful of the mixture between the palms of your hands to make a ball. Repeat until all the turkey mixture has been rolled into balls. Refrigerate for 10 minutes.

4. Heat a large saucepan and melt 1 teaspoon of oil. Add the remaining onion and garlic and sauté for a few minutes. Add the mushrooms and leek and stir. Once the leek has softened, add the tinned tomatoes and stir well, then add the vinegar and the remaining tomato purée and season.

5. Melt 1 teaspoon of oil in a frying pan over a high heat. Put the meatballs in the pan and sear for a few minutes on each side until browned, then tip them into a large casserole dish and pour over the tomato sauce. Bake for about 40 minutes.

6. Just before the meatballs have finished cooking, blanch the courgetti for a few minutes, until soft.

7. Serve the meatballs on a bed of courgetti with a sprinkling of Parmesan.

TURKEY AND RED PEPPER TRAY BAKE *Serves 4–6*

Ingredients

500g turkey breast meat
3 carrots, chopped
3 garlic cloves
2 courgettes, chopped
2 red peppers, deseeded and chopped
3 lemon thyme sprigs
1 rosemary sprig
zest and juice of 1 lemon
1 teaspoon sumac
a drizzle of olive oil
sea salt and freshly ground black pepper

Method

1. Preheat the oven to 200°C/gas mark 6.
2. Place the turkey and vegetables in a roasting tray and tuck the rosemary and thyme underneath so they don't burn in the oven. Sprinkle the lemon zest and juice and the sumac over the top and season with salt and pepper. Drizzle with olive oil.
3. Cook for 30–40 minutes or until the turkey is cooked through.

SWEET AND SOUR CHICKEN *Serves 4*

I love the idea of taking dishes that are typically unhealthy and putting a Clean and Lean spin on them.

Ingredients

1 whole chicken
3cm-piece fresh ginger, grated
a handful of coriander, chopped
a handful of parsley, chopped
2 red peppers, deseeded and chopped
2 yellow peppers, deseeded and chopped
4 red onions, quartered
1 pineapple, peeled and cut into chunks
1 red chilli, deseeded and chopped
2 tablespoons olive oil
1 tablespoon honey
6 tablespoons balsamic vinegar
1 tablespoon tamari
sea salt and freshly ground black pepper
cooked quinoa or salad, to serve

Method

1. Preheat the oven to 180°C/gas mark 4.
2. Season the chicken with salt and pepper and stuff the cavity with the grated ginger, coriander and parsley.
3. Place the peppers and onions in a casserole dish. Add the pineapple, chilli and 1 tablespoon of the oil. Mix and season well.
4. Lay the chicken on top of the pepper mixture and pour the remaining oil over the top. Cook for about 1½ hours, until cooked through and the thigh bones can easily be pulled away from the body of the bird. Remove from the oven.
5. Tip half the vegetables onto a plate with the chicken on top.
6. Transfer the remaining vegetable mixture into a food-processor with the honey, balsamic vinegar and tamari and blend to make a sauce. Add a little boiling water if it's too thick. Season to taste.
7. Carve the chicken and serve with the vegetables, a spoonful of sauce and a portion of quinoa or salad.

APPLE CIDER TURKEY WINGS *Serves 4*

If you can't get turkey wings then chicken wings are just as good. Serve this with some brown rice and steamed greens and you have a mighty dinner on your hands!

Ingredients

4 tablespoons olive oil

2 garlic cloves, peeled

1 teaspoon chilli flakes or 1 small

fresh chilli, finely chopped

1 teaspoon paprika

1 teaspoon Himalayan pink salt

½ teaspoon black pepper

4 large turkey wings

70ml apple cider vinegar

Method

1. Preheat the oven to 180°C/gas mark 4.

2. Put the olive oil, garlic, chilli, paprika and some salt and pepper in a pestle and mortar and grind together until combined.

3. Put the turkey wings in a baking dish and, with your hands, coat the wings in the marinade. Cover with foil and bake for about 1 hour.

4. Remove the dish from the oven and carefully remove the foil. Discard any juices in the dish and pour the cider vinegar over the turkey. Replace the foil and cook for another 30 minutes, then remove the foil and cook for a final 5 minutes uncovered.

TURKEY KOFTAS WITH QUINOA AND GRAPEFRUIT SALAD *Serves 1–2*

Ingredients
For the turkey koftas

150g turkey mince

6 dried apricots, finely chopped

⅛ onion, finely diced

2 sprigs oregano, picked and

finely chopped

40g quinoa flakes

sea salt

olive oil, for frying

For the grapefruit salad

2 blood oranges

2 large fennel bulbs

4 large handfuls of watercress

2 handfuls of peas or mange tout

a large handful of Brazil nuts

a drizzle of olive oil

Method

1. Line a baking tray with baking paper.

2. Place all the ingredients for the koftas in a medium-sized bowl and mix thoroughly. Wet your hands and roll tablespoons of the mixture between the palms of your hands into small meatballs. Place on the lined tray and refrigerate for 1 hour.

3. When the meatballs have almost finished chilling, make the grapefruit salad. Peel and slice one of the blood oranges into circles, reserving a slice or two for the dressing. Peel and chop the other orange and tip the pieces into a large serving bowl with all the other ingredients. Squeeze the juice of the reserved orange slices over the salad.

4. Heat a little olive oil in a frying pan and fry the meatballs until cooked through and golden brown all over.

5. Drizzle the salad with olive oil, sprinkle with sea salt, toss and serve alongside the hot meatballs.

Top tip!
Fennel has a sweet,
liquorice-like
flavour and is
beneficial for bone
and heart health.

TURMERIC TURKEY BURGERS WITH PICKLED COURGETTES *Serves 6–8*

Ingredients
For the turkey burger

1kg turkey mince

½ onion, finely chopped

1 garlic clove, grated or
finely chopped

1 free-range egg, lightly beaten

50g quinoa flakes

half a bunch of chopped
fresh parsley

1½ teaspoons turmeric

1 teaspoon cumin seeds,
lightly toasted

a pinch of cayenne pepper

2 tablespoons extra virgin olive oil
or coconut oil

sea salt and freshly ground
black pepper

For the pickled
courgettes
(makes more than you need)

1kg courgettes, finely sliced

25g salt

500ml apple cider vinegar

1 teaspoon celery seeds

1 teaspoon mustard seeds

1 teaspoon ground turmeric

½ teaspoon chilli flakes

½ teaspoon dry mustard

½ teaspoon fennel seeds

Method

1. To make the courgette pickle, put the courgette slices in a bowl and cover with water. Add the salt and let it stand for about an hour, then drain and put the courgette back in the bowl.

2. Put the remaining ingredients into a large saucepan and bring to the boil. Pour the hot mixture over the courgette and let it stand for another hour.

3. Tip the courgettes and pickles back into the saucepan, bring to the boil and cook for about 3 minutes. Set aside and cool enough of the pickle for your burgers. Pack the rest into sterilised jars, making sure there are no air bubbles, and seal.

4. Mix all the ingredients for the turkey burgers together, except the oil. Form the mixture into patties.

5. Put a frying pan over a medium heat. Rub a little oil onto both sides of the burgers and place them in the pan. Brown on each side and then sauté until cooked through and no longer pink inside, about 10 minutes.

6. Serve the burgers with the pickled courgettes on the side.

Top tip!
*Apple cider vinegar
is great for cleansing your
system. You can either
cook with it or have
a splash in a drink
of warm water
first thing.*

CHICKEN NUGGETS AND SWEET POTATO FRIES *Serves 4*

Sometimes we all crave fast food. This recipe proves you can sate all your guilty desires while remaining Clean and Lean. Not only is this a great children's option but it's great for your own inner child too.

Ingredients
For the fries

2 sweet potatoes, skin on,
cut into fries
1 tablespoon olive oil
1 teaspoon paprika
sea salt and freshly ground
black pepper

For the chicken nuggets

200g ground almonds
3 tablespoons chia seeds
1 tablespoon dried rosemary
1 tablespoon dried oregano
1 tablespoon dried basil
1 garlic clove, crushed
4 free-range eggs, beaten
4 (preferably organic) chicken
breasts, chopped into nugget-sized
pieces

Method

1. Preheat the oven to 180°C/gas mark 4. Line 2 baking trays with foil.

2. Tip the sweet potatoes onto one of the lined trays and toss in the olive oil, paprika, salt and pepper. Bake for about 30 minutes, turning halfway through cooking.

3. While the fries are cooking, mix the almonds, chia seeds, dried herbs, garlic and some salt and pepper in a bowl. Pour the mixture onto a large plate.

4. Dip each chicken piece into the beaten egg and then toss the pieces in the almond mixture. If you want your nuggets to be really crispy, it is a good idea to double dip them.

5. Place the chicken nuggets on another foil-lined baking tray. Bake in the oven for about 15–20 minutes, turning halfway through. The nuggets and fries taste delicious with the roasted red pepper dip (see page 186).

CHICKPEA-STUFFED TURKEY ROAST *Serves 4*

Ingredients

1 small turkey, about 2kg

5cm piece of fresh turmeric, grated

2 tablespoons raw honey

1 x 400g tin chickpeas, rinsed
and strained

1 garlic clove, crushed

1 rosemary sprig

a small handful of parsley

1½ lemons

1 onion, quartered

250ml vegetable stock

olive oil

sea salt and freshly ground
black pepper

Method

1. Preheat the oven to 200°C/gas mark 6.

2. Wash the turkey and pat dry. Rub half the turmeric and all the honey into the skin and season with salt and pepper.

3. Put the chickpeas, garlic, rosemary, parsley and the juice of 1 of the lemons into a food processor and blitz. Season with salt and pepper and then stuff the turkey with the mixture, finishing with the lemon half to seal the hole.

4. Place the onion quarters in the bottom of a baking dish and place the turkey on top. Bake for 45–60 minutes, basting every 10 minutes with 3–4 tablespoons of the vegetable stock. Remove from the oven.

5. Rest the turkey for half the cooking time again before serving.

Top tip!
Turmeric, a beautiful, yellow spice, can reduce inflammation in the system, soothe your stomach, help with indigestion and even fight colds and flu.

CHILLI CON CARNE _Serves 6–8_

The longer you can cook this over a low heat, the better it will taste. However, it can be done in 20 minutes if you are in a hurry. It always tastes better the next day so make it in big batches. Other serving options include with a baked sweet potato or on a bed of quinoa or lentils.

Ingredients

1 onion, diced
1 tablespoon cumin seeds
1 red chilli, deseeded and
finely chopped
3 garlic cloves, crushed
1kg lamb mince
2 red peppers, deseeded and
chopped into small pieces
1 tablespoon ground cinnamon
2 tablespoons hot chilli powder
2 x 400g tins chopped tomatoes
5 tablespoons Worcestershire sauce
1 teaspoon sugar
1 x 750g tin kidney beans
olive oil
sea salt
baby spinach and guacamole,
to serve

Method

1. Heat some oil in a large pan over a medium heat and sweat the onions with a pinch of salt for a few minutes. Add the cumin seeds and cook for a minute to release their flavour, then add the fresh chilli and garlic and cook for another minute.

2. Add the mince and cook until brown. Add the peppers, the remaining spices and salt to taste, followed by the tinned tomatoes, Worcestershire sauce and sugar, and turn the heat up to a boil.

3. Put the beans in a pan of cold water and bring to the boil. As soon as the mixture starts to boil, turn down the heat and simmer for about 10 minutes, stirring every now and then. After 10 minutes drain the beans and add them to the chilli. Continue to cook for 5 minutes.

4. Remember to taste and add more or less salt or spices accordingly. Serve on a large bed of baby spinach with some guacamole on the side.

LIVER FRY-UP _Serves 4–6_

Ingredients

1 lamb's liver
2 onions, finely sliced
a pinch of wholemeal flour
500ml white wine or apple cider
8 sage leaves, torn
2 knobs of butter
sea salt and freshly ground
black pepper
olive oil, for frying

Method

1. Rinse the lamb's liver and pat it dry with a paper towel.

2. Heat a little oil in a frying pan over a medium heat and gently sauté the onions until golden, then remove with a slotted spoon. Add another drizzle of oil to the pan.

3. Lightly flour the livers, season with salt and pepper, then sear on both sides in the pan. Remove and keep warm.

4. To make the sauce, tip out any excess oil from the pan and add the wine or cider, and the torn sage leaves. Cook the liquid down, stirring frequently, until reduced by at least half. Then add the butter, seared livers and softened onions. Gently cook until the butter has melted, turning the livers once. Don't overcook the livers or they will taste exactly how you don't want them to. Serve drizzled with the sauce.

SHEPHERD'S PIE *Serves 8*

Try making this mash with parsnip and swede in the winter or roast a cauliflower and soften it in a blender. If you are looking for a more filling option, use half sweet potato and half squash.

Ingredients

For the mash

1 large butternut squash, peeled
and cut into chunks
2 garlic cloves, peeled
1 tablespoon coconut oil, melted
125ml almond milk or rice milk
1 teaspoon dried rosemary
½ teaspoon ground nutmeg
sea salt and freshly ground
black pepper

For the filling

3 onions, chopped
3 garlic cloves, crushed
3 celery sticks, chopped
4 chestnut mushrooms, chopped
800g turkey mince
1 tablespoon dried rosemary
3 thyme sprigs, leaves removed
and stalks discarded
1 tablespoon tomato purée
2 tablespoons tamari
3 tablespoons Worcestershire sauce
2 x 400g tins chopped tomatoes
olive oil, for frying

Method

1. Preheat the oven to 180°C/gas mark 4. Line a baking tray with foil.

2. Put the squash and the garlic on the lined baking tray and drizzle with the melted coconut oil. Roast for about 30 minutes, until the squash has softened.

3. Meanwhile, get started on the filling. Heat a deep frying pan or skillet over a medium heat and add the olive oil. Once hot, add the onions and garlic and sauté until softened. Add the celery and mushrooms and stir.

4. Next add the turkey mince and use a fork to make sure the meat is broken into small pieces. Add the rosemary, thyme, tomato purée, tamari, Worcestershire sauce and seasoning. After a few minutes stir in the chopped tomatoes and lower the heat to a simmer. Continue to cook for about 20 minutes.

5. Once the squash has cooked, transfer it to a food processor along with the roasted garlic, milk, rosemary, nutmeg and pepper and blitz until smooth. Season with salt and pepper.

6. Pour the mince into a casserole dish and spoon the butternut squash mash on top, flattening it with a fork and making ridges with the prongs that will crisp up in the oven. Bake for about 30 minutes, and serve with some fresh greens.

Top tip!
Use up all your leftover veggies in your mince sauce, it's a great way to get veg haters to up their daily dose!

LAMB BOLOGNESE *Serves 4–6*

This is our go-to family meal. I love to let Charlotte (our daughter), sprinkle over any herbs she likes while it cooks on the hob – we have a little chef in the making!

Ingredients

1 onion, chopped

400g lamb mince

2 celery sticks, finely chopped

1 carrot, finely chopped

1 garlic clove, finely chopped

200g mushrooms, sliced

1 x 400g tin chopped tomatoes

400ml vegetable stock

3cm piece fresh turmeric, grated, or 1 teaspoon ground

2 sprigs oregano, leaves separated

a drizzle of olive oil

sea salt and freshly ground black pepper

4 courgettes, spiralised

Method

1. Heat the olive oil in a large frying pan over a medium heat. Add the onion and cook for a few minutes until soft.
2. Add the vegetables and continue to cook for 5 minutes until soft.
3. Add the mince and stir until browned. Now add the tomatoes and stock, oregano, turmeric and seasoning.
4. Cook for 20–25 minutes or until the sauce thickens and the lamb has cooked through.
5. Stir the courgetti through the sauce and serve topped with the bolognese.

LAMB SUMMER STEW *Serves 3*

For those on the go, there is simply not enough time to stand over a hob for half a day. However, this stew tastes like it has been and yet is ready in just over an hour: the trick is to steam the vegetables before cooking them on the hob as it speeds the whole process up without diminishing the taste. It's wonderful, nourishing and delicious and I'm sure you will love it. Please let me know what you think (unless you don't like it, in which case, keep it to yourself!).

Ingredients

750g lamb neck fillet, chopped into chunks

1 onion, chopped

leaves from 4 rosemary sprigs, plus 1 whole sprig

1 sweet potato, chopped

a bunch of spring carrots, chopped

about 12 asparagus spears, chopped

3 celery sticks, chopped

500ml lamb or vegetable stock (if you can't get fresh use an organic powder)

Method

1. Place the lamb, onion and rosemary in a large frying pan over a high heat and sear the lamb for about 2–3 minutes until golden brown all over. Remove from the heat and tip into a casserole dish.
2. Steam the veg for about 10 minutes until slightly softened, then add to the casserole dish with the meat.
3. Pour over the stock, mix well and then cook on the hob over a low heat for at least 1 hour.
4. Serve in a big bowl with a sprig of rosemary on top and season well.

GRILLED STEAK WITH ROASTED TOMATOES AND ONION *Serves 2*

A good-quality steak is a fantastic source of iron and protein. Make sure you choose a lean piece of meat and, if you can, please try and buy grass-fed and organic meat.

Ingredients

12 tomatoes on the vine

1 red onion, quartered

4 garlic cloves, sliced

1 tablespoon olive oil

1 tablespoon balsamic vinegar

a generous pinch of coarse salt

1 tablespoon coconut oil

2 sirloin steaks (250g per steak- as short and thick as possible)

a handful of pine nuts

2 handfuls of rocket

Method

1. Preheat the oven to 140°C/gas mark 1.

2. Place the tomatoes, onion and garlic on a roasting tray and drizzle with olive oil, balsamic vinegar and salt. Cook for about 40 minutes until deliciously caramelised. Leave to cool.

3. Heat a non-stick frying pan with coconut oil. Once sizzling, add the steaks and sear them on either side for about 3–4 minutes. (If you'd like the steak to be cooked medium-rare, press the tip of your middle finger to the tip of your thumb, your steak should feel similar to that).

4. Leave the steak to rest for about the same amount of time you cooked it for.

5. While the steak is resting, toast the pine nuts in the frying pan until golden brown.

6. Serve the steak with equal amounts of rocket and the warm tomato and onion mix. Sprinkle with pine nuts and drizzle with oil. Simple but seriously satisfying!

RAINBOW BURGERS *Serves 1–2*

This is a perfect source of protein for vegetarians and also a favourite with my kids; it's another great way of getting them to eat vegetables. Serve with some sweet potato fries, see page 161.

Ingredients

100g cooked quinoa

1 courgette, grated

1 small beetroot, grated

1 carrot, grated

25g Parmesan cheese, grated

a handful of baby spinach, chopped

1 tablespoon fresh turmeric, grated

1 small egg, lightly whisked

¼ teaspoon cayenne pepper

sea salt

Method

1. Place all the ingredients in a mixing bowl and stir to combine thoroughly.

2. Form the mixture into patties. If it's too wet, add some quinoa flakes or a gluten-free flour to help bind it.

3. Heat a frying pan over a high heat. Sear the patties on one side until golden, then flip them to sear the other side. Reduce the heat to medium and continue to cook for 3–4 minutes until cooked through.

Your Dinner
BAD, BETTER & BEST TABLES

BAD	BETTER	BEST
Sweet and sour chicken with egg-fried rice This is a highly processed, nutritionally empty meal. Most cheap Chinese takeaways use a huge amount of sugar in the dishes which will leave you drained, stressed and hungry.	**Chicken stir-fry with pre-chopped vegetables, sauce and basmati rice** A homemade stir-fry is always a more Clean and Lean option. However, prepared vegetables do not have the same nutritional quality as fresh produce.	**Sweet and Sour Chicken (page 157) with quinoa** Packed with fresh wonderful flavours, it might take a bit more time than ordering a takeaway but your body will thank you for it. If possible, try and buy organic chicken or at least free range.
Chicken korma with naan The average chicken korma contains over 3g more saturated fat than you are meant to eat in a day. Look after your cholesterol and step away from this dish.	**Tandoori chicken with rice** The healthiest takeaway option is a sauce-free one. Such as tandoori or tikka.	**James' Mum's Chicken Curry (page 142)** I have grown up eating this nourishing curry. Make a big batch of this and freeze it in portion sizes. It's just as easy as ordering a takeaway but will leave you feeling much happier.
Spaghetti bolognese Wheat-based pastas contain gluten, which many people are intolerant to and we generally eat too much of.	**Gluten-free pasta with meatballs** Gluten-free pasta will feel less irritating on the gut, however it's highly processed and still contains the same amount of carbohydrates as regular pasta. Being gluten free doesn't always mean it's healthier. Try and find brown rice or quinoa pasta.	**Turkey Meatballs with Courgetti (page 155)** We know that courgetti is no substitute for that pasta craving you may get. However it's much healthier and you will feel better going to bed with courgetti in your belly.
Supermarket Frozen Pizza Highly processed, minimal nutrient value and high GI – a recipe for weight gain.	**Sourdough or wholemeal pizza with fresh vegetable topping** Sourdough can be a little easier to digest. However this is still not going to fill you with the nutrients you deserve. It does makes a great cheat meal though!	**Easy Peasy Chickpea Pizza (page 107)** Try this before you slate it. It's gluten free, high in protein and a really affordable flour. You might see chickpea flour named as gram flour in supermarkets.

Dinner is the time to share delicious food with the people you love so it really is a shame to go for a nutritiously empty takeaway or ready meal. Cooking someone dinner is such a wonderful gift to give and the table below shows you how easy it is to make healthy choices.

BAD	BETTER	BEST
Takeaway fish and chips This is best avoided for many reasons. With minimal nutrients in the fish itself, no greens at all (except for maybe some mushy peas), and a load of batter and potato – this is not going to nourish your body.	**Home cooked frozen fish and chips** This is better than a takeaway because you can fry the fish in coconut oil or butter, or even better, bake it. The starchy chips and pre-frozen fish are still very low in nutrients.	**Grilled fresh fish with sweet potato fries** Increased beta-carotene and vitamin A levels are just some of the many benefits of eating sweet potato. Take a risk and buy a wild fish from your fishmonger.
Macaroni cheese Food should be colourful; that should tell you everything about the lack of goodness in this classic comfort food.	**Brown rice macaroni with broccoli, red onions, tomatoes and Parmesan** Fry some chopped onion, tomatoes and mix in the pasta and boiled brocoli. Grill with some Parmesan sprinkled on top – easy and much more nutritious.	**Quinoa pasta with homemade tomato sauce and a sprinkle of Parmesan** Fresh tomato sauce is so easy to make and is much better for you. Opt for some organic Parmesan and you have a delicious Clean and Lean meal ready to go.
Soy burger with bread roll and fries High trans-fat content and full of pesticides that can be toxic.	**Quorn burger in a wholegrain roll with a mixed salad** A much better source of protein and a healthy dose of fibre too.	**Tempeh burger (no roll) with some roasted vegetables** A fantastic nutrient-dense source of proteins and the vegetables will give you a dose of fibre too.
Pot of Noodles This is a hugely over processed, poor-quality excuse for food.	**Beef and vegetable stir fry with noodles** A good combination of vegetables and protein, but choose buckwheat noodles for added health benefits.	**Salmon or chicken stir-fry with courgette noodles** If possible, choose organic ingredients.
Vegetable curry with white rice White rice combined with a sweet curry sauce will cause your blood sugar levels to soar, making you crave more sugar	**Vegetable curry with brown rice and cumin** Brown rice is much more nutrient-dense and adding cumin is a great way of relieving digestive issues.	**Coconut Lentil Curry (page 142)** Lentils are an excellent source of protein for vegetarians and are a great gluten free choice.

chapter 7

Snacks, Sides and Extras

CARROT, BEET AND KALE CRISPS *Serves 2–4*

The crispiness of the vegetables will not last for more than a few hours so this is more of an instant snack than one you can make in advance (which is rarely an issue as they get eaten up very quickly)!

Ingredients
100g kale
2 carrots, thinly sliced into rounds
2 beetroots, thinly sliced into rounds
1 tablespoon tamari
1 teaspoon ground turmeric
1 teaspoon ground cumin
1 teaspoon mild chilli powder
freshly ground black pepper

Method
1. Preheat the oven to 150°C/gas mark 2.
2. Place the kale on a foil-lined baking tray and the carrots and beetroot together on a separate foil-lined tray.
3. Mix the tamari, turmeric, cumin, chilli powder and pepper together in a small bowl.
4. Sprinkle the spice mix equally over both baking trays and massage it into the veggies with your hands.
5. Place the beetroot and carrot in the oven for about 30 minutes turning halfway.
6. Place the kale in the oven for 15 minutes, until it becomes perfectly crispy.
7. Once both are cooked, pour into a bowl and tuck in! I love dipping them into the Baba Ganoush dip (see page 186).

PARSNIP AND CELERIAC FRIES *Serves 4*

Ingredients
4 parsnips, peeled and sliced into fries
1 small celeriac, peeled and sliced into fries
1 tablespoon coconut oil, melted
1 tablespoon rosemary
sea salt and freshly ground black pepper

Method
1. Preheat the oven to 150°C/gas mark 2.
2. Arrange the root vegetables on a baking tray.
3. Mix the oil with the rosemary and pour over the fries. Mix well with your hands and then season generously.
4. Place in the oven for about 30 minutes, until the fries look crispy and delicious.
5. Serve with a big helping of Guacamole (see page 184)!

INDIAN-SPICED CARROT CHIPS *Serves 4*

These carrots make a perfect addition to the Coconut Lentil Curry (see page 142).

Ingredients

10 carrots, cut into thin chips
1 tablespoon coconut oil, melted
2 tablespoons nigella seeds
1 teaspoon ground coriander
sea salt and freshly ground
black pepper

Method

1. Preheat the oven to 180°C/gas mark 4. Line a baking tray with foil and put it in the oven to heat up.

2. Put the carrot chips in a mixing bowl. In a separate small bowl, mix the melted oil with the nigella seeds and ground coriander. Pour this over the carrots and mix it well with your hands. Season with salt and pepper.

3. Tip the chips onto the hot baking tray and spread them out evenly. Bake for about 30 minutes, turning the carrots halfway through cooking.

SEED CRACKERS *Serves 8*

These are fire crackers; they will fill you with energy and are an ideal snack to whip up before an afternoon meeting or whenever you need an extra boost between meals.

Ingredients

175g ground almonds
50g ground flaxseed
50g pumpkin seeds
50g chia seeds
1 free-range egg, beaten
3 tablespoons coconut oil, melted
½ teaspoon sea salt
¼ teaspoon bicarbonate of soda

Method

1. Preheat the oven to 180°C/gas mark 4. Line a baking tray with baking paper.

2. Put all the ingredients in a mixing bowl and stir to combine. Form the dough into a big ball with your hands and put it on the lined baking tray. Roll out the dough (or you can just flatten it using your hands) until it's about 2cm thick.

3. Bake for 15–20 minutes until the crackers are firm and beginning to turn golden at the edges. Keep an eye on it as once it cooks it takes seconds to burn. Remove from the oven, cool on the tray and then break into pieces. (If you prefer straight and precise pieces, cut squares into the dough before baking.)

NORI WRAPS *Serves 1*

Ingredients

1 sheet of nori
2 tablespoons hummus (try it
with our Butternut Squash and
Coriander Hummus on page 182)
a handful of beansprouts
2 carrots, grated
½ cucumber, cut into thin slices
¼ avocado, peeled and sliced thinly
6 cashews, toasted and chopped
1 tablespoon tamari
1 bunch coriander, chopped
1 tablespoon lemon juice
sea salt and freshly ground
black pepper

For the dipping sauce:

3 tablespoons tahini
1 tablespoon miso
1 tablespoon tamari
1 tablespoon lime
1 teaspoon maple syrup
1 tablespoon water

Method

1. To make the sauce, simply mix all the ingredients in a food processor and pour into a small bowl.

2. Lay the nori sheet with the long edge facing you.

3. Spread the hummus over the sheet. Layer on the beansprouts, carrots, cucumber and avocado on the bottom third of the sheet. Sprinkle with cashews, tamari, coriander and lemon juice. Season to taste.

4. Gently roll the edge closest to you towards the centre of the nori wrap (just like a sushi roll). With a sharp knife, slice your roll and serve with the sauce.

QUINOA AND CAROB BALLS *Serves 10–12*

Ingredients

200g quinoa
1 tablespoon coconut oil
100g pitted dates, roughly chopped
½ teaspoon ground cinnamon
50g mixed nuts, finely chopped
(optional)
2 tablespoons honey or maple
syrup
2 tablespoons nut butter
1 tablespoon carob powder
50g shredded or flaked coconut
(not desiccated as it often has
sugar added)

Method

1. Rinse the quinoa well and put it in a saucepan over a medium heat with double the amount of boiling water. Cook for about 10 minutes, until the grain unwraps itself but still has a slight crunch. Drain, add the coconut oil and stir until it's melted, then set aside to cool.

2. Add all the other ingredients to the cooked quinoa, except the flaked coconut.

3. Divide the mixture into 10g portions and roll between the palms of your hands into balls. Roll in the coconut to coat.

4. Leave to set in the fridge for 2 hours or overnight.

CAYENNE AND WASABI BAKED CHICKPEAS *Serves 12–14*

These hot chickpeas are a great pre-dinner snack. If you like it spicy, then definitely give these a go.

Ingredients

2 teaspoons butter or coconut oil
2 tablespoons wasabi powder (less if you prefer)
2 tablespoons tahini
2 tablespoons mustard powder
a pinch of cayenne pepper
a pinch of Himalayan pink salt
a pinch of paprika
a pinch of pepper
1 x 400g tin chickpeas, rinsed, loose skins discarded, and dried

Method

1. Preheat the oven to 220°C/gas mark 7. Line a baking tray with baking paper.

2. Place the butter or coconut oil in a saucepan and warm it for 2 minutes until melted. Mix all the ingredients except the chickpeas into it, then add the chickpeas and mix well to coat.

3. Pour the chickpea mixture onto the prepared baking tray and bake for 30 minutes, or until golden brown, shaking the tray every so often so the chickpeas don't stick. Remove from the oven and set aside to cool.

COURGETTE AND CARROT CRACKERS *Serves 2*

Rather than waste the pulp from our juicer, I love to experiment and work out different recipes to make with the leftover pulp. These crackers are my favourite creation so far. Feel free to try this with any other vegetables that you decide to juice. You could also make a sweet cracker with fruit, flaxseed and a spoon of raw honey.

Ingredients

2 carrots
2 courgettes
3 tablespoons flaxseed
1 tablespoon tomato purée
1 garlic clove, crushed
2 tablespoons tamari
1 tablespoon tahini
a handful of coriander stalks, chopped
sea salt and freshly ground black pepper

Method

1. Preheat the oven to 120°C/gas mark ½.

2. If you have a juicer, juice the carrots and courgettes and place the pulp of the vegetables in a mixing bowl (drink or discard the juice). For those that don't have a juicer, grate the vegetables into a bowl.

3. Add the rest of the ingredients and mix well.

4. Pour the mixture into a baking tray and, using a rolling pin, flatten the mix as thinly as possible.

5. Place in the oven for about 35 minutes. Halfway through baking, use a knife and slice the mixture into cracker-sized pieces. Turn over half way through cooking.

6. Once hard, remove from the oven and leave to cool. We love to dip these in the Baba Ganoush dip (see page 186)!

GRIDDLED CORN AND TOASTED COCONUT *Serves 4*

This is such an easy side for warm summer evenings. Rather than slathering heaps of salt and butter on your corn, try a tropical twist on this classic barbecue dish.

Ingredients
2 handfuls of coconut chips
4 corn cobs
1 lime, quartered
coconut oil, for grilling

Method
1. Preheat the oven to 180°C/gas mark 4.
2. Lay the coconut chips on a baking tray and toast in the oven for a few minutes until golden brown.
3. Heat some oil in a griddle pan over a high heat. Add the corn and cook for about 10 minutes, turning every few minutes. Remove from the pan.
4. Squeeze the lime over the corn and sprinkle with toasted coconut chips.

BUTTERNUT SQUASH AND CORIANDER HUMMUS *Serves 6*

Ingredients
1 butternut squash, peeled and chopped
1 lemon, juiced
2 garlic cloves
2 tablespoons tahini
a handful of coriander stalks
sea salt and freshly ground black pepper
olive oil, to drizzle
coriander leaves, to serve

Method
1. Preheat the oven to 180°C/gas mark 4. Place the squash on a baking tray and roast for about 30 minutes until tender. Leave to cool.
2. Once the squash is cool, place in a food processor with the lemon juice, garlic, tahini, coriander and some salt and pepper. Blitz until smooth.
3. Pour into a small bowl and drizzle with olive oil and sprinkle with some coriander leaves.
4. This tastes delicious with the Carrot and Courgette Crackers (see page 181).

PEA AND BROAD BEAN SMASH *Serves 2*

Ingredients
200g broad beans, blanched

100g peas, blanched, or thawed
if frozen

1 small red onion, finely diced

a small handful of mint leaves

1 tablespoon apple cider vinegar

a dash of olive oil

100g ricotta

sea salt and freshly ground
black pepper

Method
1. Pulse the beans and peas in a food processor until just chopped.

2. Add the onion, mint, vinegar and oil and blitz again. Transfer the mixture to a bowl.

3. Mix in the ricotta and season to taste.

GUACAMOLE *Serves 6–8*

This makes a good side for the Chilli Con Carne (see page 165) or a delicious spread if you have any leftover.

Ingredients
2 ripe avocados, peeled, stoned
and chopped

zest and juice of 1 lemon or lime

1 small red chilli, deseeded and
finely chopped

2 spring onions or ½ red onion,
finely diced

a drizzle of olive oil

sea salt

Method
1. Put the avocado into a bowl with the lemon or lime zest and juice. Add the chopped chilli, onions, a generous drizzle of olive oil and salt to taste.

2. Mash lightly with a fork to your preferred consistency.

ROASTED RED PEPPER DIP *Serves 6–8*

As well as being a very popular dip for crudités, this is also perfect served alongside the Quinoa Tabbouleh (see page 104).

Ingredients
4 red peppers
1 small onion, chopped
1 garlic clove, crushed
1 tablespoon tahini
1 tablespoon red wine vinegar
juice of 1 lemon
a handful of coriander
a handful of parsley
sea salt and freshly ground black pepper
coconut oil, for frying

Method
1. Preheat the oven to 180°C/gas mark 4. Line a baking tray with foil.
2. Place the peppers on the baking tray and bake until soft and slightly browned. Remove from the oven and leave to cool.
3. Heat a saucepan over a low heat and melt 1 teaspoon of oil. Add the onion and garlic and sauté for 5 minutes until softened.
4. Deseed the peppers and put them in a food-processor with the onion, garlic and the rest of the ingredients, and blitz. Season with salt and pepper.

BABA GANOUSH *Serves 6–8*

Ingredients
3 aubergines
juice of 1 lemon
1 tablespoon olive oil
1 tablespoon water
1 tablespoon tahini
1 garlic clove, crushed
sea salt and freshly ground black pepper

Method
1. Preheat the oven to 200°C/gas mark 6. Line a baking tray with foil.
2. Using a knife, slit the aubergine skins all over and then place them on the baking tray on the top shelf of the oven. Cook for about 15 minutes, until the aubergines have softened all the way through, turning once. Remove and set aside to cool slightly.
3. Put the aubergines in a bowl of cold water and use a knife to peel off the skins. Roughly chop the aubergine flesh and put it in a food-processor with the rest of the ingredients. Blitz until smooth and season well with salt and pepper.

OLIVE, PINE NUT AND ROCKET SALAD *Serves 4*

When we have friends round for a dinner party, I love to create an atmosphere for sharing, so along with a main course, I like to rustle up some sides for guests to help themselves to at the table. It makes it feel less formal and means that everyone can share and enjoy the food together.

Ingredients

20 vine tomatoes
2 garlic cloves, sliced
3 tablespoons balsamic vinegar
100g rocket
100g green olives, pitted and sliced
a handful of pine nuts, toasted
olive oil and balsamic vinegar,
to serve
sea salt and freshly ground
black pepper

Method

1. Preheat the oven to 150°C/gas mark 2. Place the tomatoes and garlic on a baking tray and drizzle with the balsamic vinegar. Place in the oven for about 20 minutes until the tomato skins have softened.

2. In a salad bowl, mix the rocket and olives. Once the tomatoes have cooled, pour them into the salad bowl with the toasted pine nuts.

3. Drizzle over some olive oil and a splash of balsamic vinegar and season well before serving.

ROOT SALAD *Serves 6*

This is one of my favourite salads. I have been perfecting the art of making perfect roasted roots for a while now. I love them crunchy on the outside and creamy on the inside. Add any other vegetables that are in your fridge and serve this on the table with any main to make a delicious, colourful dinner.

Ingredients

½ butternut squash, peeled
and chopped
3 carrots, sliced lengthways
and quartered
2 beetroot, chopped, skin on
2 tablespoons coconut oil, melted
a handful of pecans, chopped
4 handfuls of rocket
sea salt and freshly ground
black pepper

For the dressing

juice of 1 lemon
1 garlic clove, crushed
3 tablespoons tahini
2 tablespoons extra virgin olive oil
1 tablespoon maple syrup
1 tablespoon apple cider vinegar

Method

1. Preheat the oven to 180°C/gas mark 4. Put the chopped root vegetables onto a lined baking tray, drizzle the melted coconut oil over the top and season with salt and pepper.

2. Bake the vegetables for about 30 minutes, until cooked through.

3. Tip the pecans onto a separate baking tray and toast in the oven for a few minutes, until they start to brown. Remove from the oven and set aside.

4. Put all the ingredients for the dressing in a small bowl and mix well. Season with salt and pepper.

5. Tip the roasted vegetables into a salad bowl with the rocket. When you are ready to serve, pour the dressing over the salad, toss to mix and sprinkle with the toasted pecans.

FRIDGE KRAUT *Serves 30*

Ingredients

½ medium head green cabbage,
outer leaves discarded
1 tablespoon sea salt
1 tablespoon mixed caraway,
celery, cumin, dill, fennel or
mustard seeds, chilli flakes, dried
ginger or dried turmeric (optional)

Method

1. Clean everything! When fermenting, it's best to give the good, beneficial bacteria every chance of succeeding by starting off with as clean an environment as possible. Give your hands a good wash too.

2. Reserve 1 big outer leaf, then cut the cabbage into quarters and trim out the core. Slice each quarter to make 8 wedges and then slice each wedge across into very thin strips. Put the cabbage into a big mixing bowl and sprinkle the salt over the top.

3. Work the salt into the cabbage by massaging and squeezing it with your hands. Gradually the cabbage will become watery and limp – more like coleslaw than raw cabbage. This will take about 5 minutes.

4. Add the flavourings, if using.

5. Pack the cabbage tightly into a steralised mason jar, tamping it down with your fist every so often. Pour in any liquid released while you were massaging it into the jar.

6. Place the reserved leaf over the surface of the sliced cabbage, then slip a smaller jam jar into the mouth of the mason jar and weigh it down with clean stones or marbles.

7. Cover the mouth of the jar with a cloth and secure it with a rubber band or twine. This will allow air to flow in and out of the jar, but stop dust or insects getting in.

8. Over the next 24 hours, press down on the cabbage every so often with the jam jar. As the cabbage releases its liquid, it will become more limp and compact and the liquid will rise over the top of the cabbage.

9. If after 24 hours the liquid has not risen above the cabbage, dissolve 1 teaspoon of salt in 250ml water and add enough to submerge the cabbage.

10. Ferment the cabbage at a cool room temperature – ideally 18°C–23°C – away from direct sunlight for 3–10 days. Check it daily and press it down if the cabbage is floating above the liquid.

11. Start tasting the kraut after 3 days – when it tastes good to you, remove the weight, screw on the cap, and refrigerate. It can ferment for 10 days or even longer. You may see bubbles rising through the cabbage, foam on the top, or white scum. These are all signs of a healthy, happy fermentation process. The scum can be skimmed off. If you see any mould, skim it off immediately and make sure your cabbage is fully submerged; don't eat mouldy parts close to the surface, but the rest of the sauerkraut is fine.

12. Sauerkraut will keep for at least 2 months and often longer if kept refrigerated. As long as it still tastes and smells good to eat, it will be.

BUTTER *Serves 20*

For some reason, butter seems to have lost popularity and many people assume it's unhealthy and stick to coconut oil and olive oil. Of course, coconut is fabulous but so is butter (as long as it's grass fed and organic). It's packed with antioxidants and minerals and what's more, it adds such great taste to so many dishes too.

Ingredients

250ml double cream at room
temperature
a pinch of sea salt (optional)
ice

Method

1. Pour the cream into a 1-litre steralised jar with the pinch of salt (if using) and add 1 glass marble.

2. Shake the jar with the marble inside for about 3 minutes. The cream will softly whip, then become stiff. Keep shaking until the buttermilk separates.

3. Tip into a sieve over a bowl and strain the buttermilk (use this for something else).

4. Tip the butter into ice-cold water and then use your hands to massage out the remaining buttermilk – you need to remove it all or it will sour the butter. Wash the butter a couple of times.

5. Add a pinch of salt and mould into whatever shape you like. Put in an airtight container or wrap in cling film and keep in the fridge for up to 2 weeks.

KIMCHI *Serves 30*

This recipe is spicy and gets spicier the longer it sits – add or subtract chilli paste to your taste.

Ingredients

1 head cabbage, about 1kg, outer
leaves removed
40g kosher salt
112ml rice vinegar
1 tablespoon brown sugar
2 tablespoons hot chilli paste
2.5cm piece fresh ginger, grated
2 garlic cloves, finely chopped
2 shallots, finely sliced

Method

1. Cut the cabbage into quarters and remove the tough inner core. Cut across the wedges to make 1cm slices.

2. Tip the cabbage into a colander, add the salt and mix well. Place the colander over a clean bowl and let the cabbage drain, weighed down by a saucepan lid or plate, until wilted, about 2 hours.

3. In a large bowl, combine the vinegar and sugar and stir to dissolve. Add the chilli paste, ginger, garlic and shallots, and stir.

4. Rinse the salt from the cabbage with a couple of changes of water. Dry well and add to the vinegar mixture, stirring well to combine.

5. Pack into a sterilized mason jar and pour in just enough water to cover. Seal the jar and refrigerate for at least 4 hours.

CHARRED BROCCOLI, WITH LEMON, GARLIC AND CHILLI *Serves 4*

I love adding chilli to my food. It's really tasty and if you only add a little and throw away the seeds it doesn't have to be that hot (of course, you can make it hotter if you like it that way).

Ingredients

600g tenderstem broccoli
1 red chilli, deseeded and finely chopped
5 garlic cloves, thinly sliced
3 tablespoons olive oil
1 lemon, zest and juice
sea salt and freshly ground black pepper
a handful flaked almonds, toasted

Method

1. Bring a saucepan of water to the boil on the hob. Add the broccoli and blanch for 2 minutes. Drain and place the broccoli in cold water (so that it stops cooking).

2. Place a griddle pan over a high heat on the hob. Once it is very hot, add the broccoli in batches and let it cook so it gets char marks all over. Once cooked, place in a salad bowl. After you have cooked all the broccoli, place the chilli and garlic in the pan, with 1 tablespoon of oil and let it char for a few minutes.

3. Add the garlic and chilli to the salad bowl. Squeeze the lemon juice into the bowl and add the zest and remaining oil. Season with salt and pepper and sprinkle with the toasted almonds.

CHRISTIANE'S RICE AND BEANS *Serves 4*

This is Christiane's speciality. Beans boost your circulation and this Brazilian recipe is my ultimate comfort food. This is a perfect Brazilian addition to a roast lamb or chicken.

Ingredients

500g black beans, dried (not from a tin)
1 teaspoon coconut oil
1 onion, chopped
3 garlic cloves, crushed
170g brown rice
1 litre chicken or vegetable stock (if you do not have fresh stock to hand use an organic stock cube)
3 bay leaves
200g kale
juice of 1 orange
sea salt and freshly ground black pepper

Method

1. Soak the beans in cold water overnight, making sure they are completely covered.

2. Pour the beans into a saucepan of cold water and bring to the boil over a medium heat. Leave to simmer for 30 minutes until tender.

3. Heat another saucepan and add the oil. Once melted, add the onion and garlic and season well. Leave to sauté for 5 minutes. Add the bay leaves, pour in the beans and add the rice. Mix well.

4. Add the stock and reduce the heat, leave to cook until the liquid has been absorbed and the rice is tender. If all the liquid absorbs before the rice is ready, add a ladle more water.

5. Stir in the kale and let it wilt before taking off the heat. Pour over the orange juice and mix well. Season to taste.

CUMIN AND GARLIC ROASTED CAULIFLOWER *Serves 4*

This tastes great with curry, or as an addition to a simple green salad.

Ingredients

1 tablespoon coconut oil, melted

1 tablespoon cumin

2 garlic cloves, crushed

1 cauliflower, outer leaves removed, cut into florets

sea salt

1 handful flaked almonds, toasted

Method

1. Preheat the oven to 180°C/gas mark 4.

2. Mix the oil with the cumin and garlic

3. Place the florets on a baking tray and pour over the oil. Season with salt and roast in the oven for about 30 minutes.

4. While the cauliflower is crisping up, place the almond flakes in the oven until they turn golden brown.

5. Just before serving, sprinkle over the toasted almonds.

ARTICHOKE, SPINACH AND TAHINI DIP *Serves 4*

This vibrant green dip is delicious with almost any main. I love to serve sweet potato fries with this or I sometimes stir it into a portion of quinoa.

Ingredients

1 teaspoon coconut oil

1 red onion

2 garlic cloves, crushed

200g spinach

240g tin artichoke hearts, drained

1 tablespoon tahini

4 tablespoons greek yogurt

1 handful fresh parsley

½ lemon, squeezed

sea salt and freshly ground black pepper

Method

1. In a frying pan, heat the coconut oil. Once melted, add the red onion and garlic and sauté for 10 minutes. Add the spinach and stir until wilted.

2. In a food processor, mix the remaining ingredients together with the spinach mixture. Pour into a bowl, cut up some crudité and enjoy!

Top tip!
Dips are a really great way of experimenting with different flavours.

CLEAN AND LEAN BREAD *Serves 4*

Ingredients
chopped red onion (optional)
a sprig of rosemary (optional)

Dry ingredients
128g coconut flour
128g ground flaxseed
128g pumpkin seeds
384g almond flour
32g poppy seeds
32g sesame seeds
7.5g baking powder
a pinch of sea salt
a pinch of black pepper
3 thyme sprigs
3 rosemary sprigs
3 tablespoons psyllium husk
(optional)

Wet ingredients
75g coconut oil, melted
5 eggs
156g rice milk
3 tablespoons apple cider vinegar
192g blended tofu

Method
1. Preheat the oven to 180°C/gas mark 4. Grease a 23x12x7cm loaf tin.
2. Mix all the dry ingredients together in a bowl. Mix the wet ingredients together in a separate bowl. Add the dry mix to the wet mixture.
3. Pour the mix into the greased tin and bake for 30 minutes.
4. Layer the red onion and rosemary, if using, on top of the bread and return to the oven for another 10–15 minutes.

Top tip!
This is a delicious tasting protein power boost – I love it straight after a work out.

SWEET POTATO SKINS WITH A TRIO OF FILLINGS *Serves 4*

Whenever we have a barbecue, I serve these filled skins as a Clean and Lean equivalent to the traditional potato skins. Get creative and make up your own fillings!

Ingredients
2 sweet potatoes

For the guacamole filling
1 avocado
1 garlic clove, crushed
½ red onion, chopped
juice of 1 lemon
a handful of fresh coriander, chopped
½ teaspoon paprika
sea salt and freshly ground black pepper

For the harissa yogurt filling
250g Greek yogurt
juice of 1 lemon
1 garlic clove, crushed
2 teaspoons harissa
1 tablespoon coriander, chopped

For the feta, sundried tomato and olive filling
60g feta, diced
30g black olives, pitted and chopped
30g sundried tomatoes, chopped
a handful of basil, chopped
1 tablespoon good-quality olive oil
1 teaspoon dried oregano

Method
1. Preheat the oven to 180°C/gas mark 4. Put a baking tray in the oven to heat up.
2. Prick the potatoes with a fork and put them on the hot baking tray in the oven. Bake for about 40 minutes, or until they can be easily pierced with a fork. Remove and leave until cool enough to handle.
3. While the potatoes are cooking, make the fillings:

To make guacamole-filled potatoes
1. Mash the avocado flesh with a fork and mix it with the rest of the ingredients.
2. Once the potatoes are cool enough to handle, slice them lengthways and scoop out the flesh, leaving a thin layer of potato on the inside.
3. Mix the sweet potato flesh with the avocado mix and season well.
4. Divide the mixture evenly between the potato skins and put them back in the oven for 5–10 minutes.

To make harissa yogurt-filled potatoes
1. Mix all the ingredients together.
2. Once the potatoes are cool enough to handle, slice them lengthways and scoop out the flesh, leaving a thin layer of potato on the inside.
3. Mix the sweet potato with the harissa yogurt mix and season well.
4. Divide the mixture evenly between the potato skins and serve.

To make feta, sundried tomato and olive-filled potatoes
1. Once the potatoes are cool enough to handle, slice them lengthways and scoop out the flesh, leaving a thin layer of potato on the inside.
2. Mix the sweet potato with all the ingredients.
3. Divide the mixture evenly between the potato skins and put back in the oven for 5–10 minutes.

TEGAN'S BITES

All these were created by Tegan, one of our top Bodyism trainers. They are a perfect pre- or post-workout snack and are loved by many of the clients we train.

Banana Protein Balls *Makes 12*

Ingredients
10g dried banana chips
50g ground almonds
25g Bodyism Vanilla Protein Excellence
20g raw cacao powder, plus extra for rolling
15ml raw honey

Method
1. Soak the banana chips in warm water for up to 1 hour until soft.
2. Put the soft banana chips into a food processor and blend. Add the remaining ingredients and blend well to combine. You may need to add 20ml boiling water if the mix is too dry.
3. Divide the mixture into 10g portions and roll into balls. Roll in some raw cacao powder to coat. Leave to set in the fridge for 2 hours or overnight.

Beauty Bites *Makes 12*

Ingredients
65g dates, pitted
45g ground cashews
10g Bodyism Beauty Food powder
desiccated coconut, for rolling

Method:
1. Soak the dates in warm water for up to 1 hour until soft.
2. Put into a food processor and blend until you have a sticky paste. Add the cashews and Beauty Food powder and blend.
3. Divide into 10g portions and roll into balls. Roll in the coconut to coat. Leave to set in the fridge for 2 hours or overnight.

Chocolate Serenity Balls *Makes 12*

Ingredients
60g dates, pitted
40g ground cashews
20g Bodyism Serenity Powder
¼ teaspoon ground cinnamon
10g raw cacao powder

Method:
1. Soak the dates in warm water for up to 1 hour until soft.
2. Put into a food processor and blend until you have a sticky paste.
3. Add the cashews, Serenity powder, cinnamon and cacao and blend.
4. Divide the mixture into 10g portions and roll into balls. Leave to set in the fridge for 2 hours or overnight.

Rosemary Cacao Balls *Makes 8–10*

Ingredients
175g dates, pitted
140g raw cashews
2 rosemary sprigs, leaves removed and finely chopped
½ teaspoon vanilla extract
1 tablespoon raw cacao powder
a pinch of Himalayan salt
a handful of sesame seeds

Method
1. Put all of the ingredients, except the sesame seeds, into a food processor and blitz until combined.
2. Divide the mixture into 10g portions and roll into balls.
3. Roll in the sesame seeds on a shallow plate to coat.
4. Leave to set in the fridge for 2 hours or overnight.

ALMOND, CINNAMON AND VANILLA BUTTER *Makes 1 jar*

This is a staple spread in the Duigan household. I spoon this on berries, add it to smoothies and spread it on Clean and Lean bread.

Ingredients
280g raw almonds
1 tablespoon coconut oil, melted
1 tablespoon ground cinnamon
1 teaspoon vanilla extract
½ teaspoon sea salt

Method
1. Preheat the oven to 180°C/gas mark 4.
2. Place the almonds on a baking tray and roast for 5–7 minutes until toasted. Remove and leave to cool. Turn off the oven.
3. Put the cooled almonds into a food processor and whizz on a medium speed for about 10 minutes until you have a paste. Stop every few minutes to scrape the nuts from the blade.
4. Add the remaining ingredients and pulse for a few more minutes.
5. Spoon the butter into a sterilised jar and seal. Serve on toast, with sliced apples, spread down the middle of a celery stick or straight out of the jar!

APPLE CRISPS WITH ALMOND BUTTER *Serves 4*

Ingredients

For the apple crisps
4 apples, such as Braeburn, very thinly sliced
1 tablespoon ground cinnamon
Almond, Cinnamon and Vanilla Butter (see above), to serve

Method
1. Preheat the oven to 150°C/gas mark 2. Line a baking tray with baking paper.
2. Lay the apples on the lined baking tray and sprinkle with the cinnamon.
3. Bake for 30 minutes, until the apples are crisp. Remove from the oven, leave to cool and serve with Almond, Cinnamon and Vanilla butter.

Top tip!
I love these crisps dipped into almond butter as a pre-workout snack.

CINNAMON AND MAPLE POPCORN

When it's movie night, snacks are essential. Rather than opt for the sugary, shop-bought popcorn, make a Clean and Lean version. If possible, opt for organic popping corn.

Ingredients

1 tablespoon coconut oil
200g popping corn kernels
1 tablespoon xylitol
1 tablespoon ground cinnamon
1 teaspoon sea salt
3 tablespoons maple syrup

Method

1. Preheat the oven to 150°C/gas mark 2.

2. Heat the oil in a large saucepan over a medium heat. Add 3 of the corn kernels and leave until they pop. Once popped, pour in the rest of the corn and stir in the oil to coat. Put the lid on the pan and shake the corn. Wait for the corn to pop. Once the popping has slowed down to several seconds between each pop, turn off the heat.

3. Once the popping has stopped completely, add the xylitol, cinnamon, salt and maple syrup and mix well. Pour the popcorn onto a large baking tray and put in the oven for 10 minutes to crisp up. Remove and leave to cool.

4. Serve in a big bowl and enjoy with friends.

CINNAMON SPICED NUTS *Serves 2–4*

Ingredients

2 tablespoons coconut oil, melted
2 teaspoons ground cinnamon
1 teaspoon ground ginger
1 teaspoon vanilla essence
a pinch of sea salt
2 handfuls of mixed nuts

Method

1. Preheat the oven to 180°C/gas mark 4. Line a baking tray with baking paper.

2. In a small bowl, mix the oil, cinnamon, ginger, vanilla essence and salt together. Add the nuts to the mix and using your hands massage the oil into the nuts.

3. Pour the nuts onto the baking tray and place in the oven for about 6–7 minutes, until golden brown. We love to eat these straight out of the oven!

Top tip!
Don't go nuts on nuts – they're great but be mindful of how many you are eating.

Your Snacks, Sides and Extras
BAD, BETTER & BEST TABLES

BAD	BETTER	BEST
A packet of crisps High levels of salt and hardly any nutritional benefits.	**Vegetable crisps** Vegetable crisps contain more vitamins and minerals. However, be cautious of the high salt content.	**Kale Crisps (page 176)** We love this glory girl of the green vegetable world. Their crunchy texture mean they're a great alternative to starchier options.
Salted nuts Packaged salted nuts can have very high salt levels and often use low quality table salt.	**Raw nuts** Unsalted nuts mean that you can control your salt type and intake. Sea and rock salt are best.	**Soaked or roasted nuts** A lot of nuts have a coating that is difficult to digest – soaking your nuts overnight and roasting them breaks down the enzymes, making them easier to digest.
Cheap chocolate bar Popular chocolate bars have high levels of sugar and preservatives.	**70% dark chocolate** Dark chocolate has much less sugar than other types of chocolate. It also contains minimal to no dairy produce.	**Raw chocolate** Without the sugar, raw chocolate is packed with wonderful properties. It is one of the greatest sources of antioxidants on the planet.
Shop-bought cookies Contain sugar and gluten and will just have you craving more sugar in no time.	**Oat biscuits** Contain fibre and only small amounts of gluten.	**Cashew and Carob Cookies (page 227)** Carob doesn't contain caffeine so it will curb those chocolate cravings without the spike in cortisol! It is also high in vitamin E – great for your skin and immune system.
Shop-bought blueberry muffin These should be called sugar bombs. Yes it may have a few blueberries in, but the artificial flavourings and huge amounts of sugar make this an unhealthy choice.	**Spelt muffin** You can find healthier versions of pre-made muffins in many health shops. This cleaner option will give you more fibre and less bad fats, but it's likely that the sugar content will still be high.	**Apple, Ginger and Blueberry Muffins (page 67)** These beauties are made with buckwheat flour and gluten-free oats which will keep your digestive tract very happy.

When hunger strikes and you're tempted to add an unhealthy extra to your dinner table like a premade dip and breadsticks, stop! Once you've seen the fun you can have making your own homemade sides and snacks, you'll never look back.

BAD	BETTER	BEST
Yogurt-coated raisins and nuts 'Yogurt-coated' is more like sugar coated; these need to be regarded as a treat rather than a healthy snack.	**Dried raisins, cranberries and sweetened nuts** These are still quite high in sugar and sulphites, ruining the vitamins in the foods they are preserving. But definitely better than a yogurt coating.	**Unsweetened raisins and nuts** The nuts will slow down the absorption of sugar into the blood, which will sate your sweet cravings.
Shop-bought cereal bar Often cereal bars are marketed as healthy; do not believe it. They are often filled with sugar and other nasties. Read the ingredients first.	**Date and nut bars** These are becoming increasingly popular in supermarkets which is a great thing. Although dates are a natural sweetener, they are high in fructose so eat these as a treat rather than a daily fix.	**Apple Crisps with Almond Butter (page 200)** This is a perfect snack. The sweetness of the apple tastes delicious with the creamy nut butter. It will give you a Clean and Lean energy boost.
Tinned peaches Canned fruit is loaded with excess sugar and the nutrient content is much lower than fresh fruit.	**Fresh peaches or nectarines with Greek yogurt** Fresh fruit is always better than buying the preserved equivalent. Greek yogurt is a great source of protein and makes this a much more filling snack.	**A fresh organic peach and a handful of nuts with coconut yogurt** Choosing organic when possible is a much better option as there is no risk of sulphite exposure. The nuts will slow the release of sugar into the bloodstream preventing cravings later in the day.
Fruit-flavoured yogurt Highly processed and packed with sugar. It will leave you hungry for more sugar.	**Natural organic yogurt and berries** Contains far less sugar and fresh berries are much better than a puréed version.	**Coconut yogurt, berries and almond butter** Coconut yogurt is a delicious dairy free equivalent and it's packed with good fats too.

chapter 8

Desserts

GRIDDLED PINEAPPLE AND COCONUT *Serves 4*

Another seriously easy post-dinner treat. Pineapple is the only known source of an enzyme called bromelain, which is used to alleviate joint pain and reduce inflammation.

Ingredients
2 handfuls of coconut chips
1 pineapple, peeled and sliced
4 scoops of coconut yogurt
ice cream

Method
1. Preheat the oven to 180°C/gas mark 4. Place the coconut chips on a baking tray and toast in the oven for a few minutes until golden brown.

2. Heat a griddle pan over a medium-high heat. Once the pan is hot, add the pineapple slices and grill for 1–2 minutes each side, until softened.

3. Serve the pineapple with a scoop of coconut yogurt ice cream, sprinkled with the toasted coconut.

ALMOND BUTTER COOKIES *Makes 8*

Nut butter and jam are the perfect pair. Sink your teeth into these crunchy and gooey cookies or dunk them into a Clean and Lean Serenity supplement shake (see page 59) before bed and enjoy the ultimate indulgence.

Ingredients
150g ground almonds
65g buckwheat flour
2 tablespoons chia seeds
½ teaspoon sea salt
1 teaspoon baking powder
225g coconut palm sugar
225g almond butter
5–6 tablespoons naturally
sweetened strawberry or
raspberry jam

Method
1. Preheat the oven to 180°C/gas mark 4. Line 2 baking trays with baking paper.

2. Put the ground almonds, buckwheat flour, chia seeds, salt and baking powder into a bowl and mix together.

3. Heat the coconut palm sugar with 125ml water in a saucepan over a low heat until the sugar is dissolved and you have a syrup. Pour into a small mixing bowl, add the almond butter and stir. Pour into the ground almond mixture and stir well to combine. Chill in the fridge for 10 minutes so that the dough firms up.

4. Roll a tablespoon of mixture between the palms of your hands to make balls and place on the lined baking tray about 4cm part. Using the back of a spoon create a small well in the centre of each cookie. Add 1 teaspoon of jam into each well.

5. Bake for 12–15 minutes, checking closely as the cookies can burn very quickly. Leave to cool on the sheet and then enjoy with our night time supplement, Serenity!

ROSEMARY-POACHED PEARS *Serves 4*

Ingredients

1 litre filtered water
4 tablespoons honey
2 rosemary sprigs
1 teaspoon cloves
1 teaspoon black peppercorns
½ lemon
4 pears (Conference or Bosc),
peeled, cored and quartered (you
can leave peel on if you wish)
crème fraîche or yogurt, to serve

Method

1. Cut a circle of baking paper the same size as your large saucepan and cut a small hole in the middle for steam to escape from.

2. Pour the water and honey into the pan over a medium heat and warm until the honey dissolves. Add the rosemary, cloves, peppercorns and the lemon.

3. Add the pears to the pan and cover with the circle of baking paper. Simmer for 20–25 minutes depending on your preferred texture.

4. Once cooked, leave the pears to sit in the poaching liquid for 20 minutes or so before serving with crème fraîche or yogurt. You can also decant into sterilised jars and store, or keep in an airtight container in the fridge for up to 1 week.

CHOCOLATE ORANGE AND AVOCADO MOUSSE *Serves 4*

For an added bonus we love to serve the mousse in espresso cups and, halfway through filling, add a layer of granola to add some crunchy texture to the chocolate delight.

Ingredients

1 banana, sliced and frozen
1 avocado, peeled and stoned
3 tablespoons cacao powder
2 scoops Bodyism Body Brilliance
(optional)
3 tablespoons maple syrup
1 teaspoon vanilla extract
a pinch of sea salt
zest and juice from ½ orange
about 4 teaspoons granola
(optional)

Method

1. Blitz the frozen banana slices and the avocado flesh in a food processor. Add the cacao powder, Body Brilliance, if using, maple syrup, vanilla extract, salt and orange juice. Blitz again.

2. Spoon the mixture into espresso cups. If you like, halfway through filling, add a sprinkling of granola, then continue to fill the cup.

3. To serve, sprinkle over the orange zest. Refrigerate until serving.

Top tip!
Avocados are a super nutritious way of adding creaminess to any dessert.

A TRIO OF CRUMBLES *Serves 8*

Ingredients
For the topping

85g blanched and roasted hazelnuts

170g quinoa or oat flakes

5 tablespoons coconut oil, melted

200g ground almonds

a handful of flaked almonds

3 tablespoons buckwheat flour

1 teaspoon vanilla extract

2 tablespoons xylitol or stevia

4 tablespoons maple syrup

a pinch of sea salt

Method

1. Preheat the oven to 150°C/gas mark 2. Line a baking tray with baking paper. Put the hazelnuts and quinoa or oat flakes into a food processor and blitz, then pour into a mixing bowl along with the rest of the ingredients. Stir well.

2. Pour the mixture onto the lined baking tray and use a spatula to pat the crumble down so that it is densely packed.

3. Bake for 15 minutes until the crumble has browned slightly. Remove and leave to cool while you make the filling of your choice.

Apple, Blueberry and Coconut

Ingredients

6 apples (such as Granny Smith, Cox, Pink Lady), cored and chopped

1 punnet blueberries

2 tablespoons desiccated coconut

1 tablespoon stevia

2 teaspoons ground cinnamon

1 teaspoon vanilla extract

juice of 1 lemon

Method

1. Place all the ingredients in a saucepan over a low heat. Add 2 tablespoons water and cook until the apple has softened.

2. Pour the mixture into ramekins or an ovenproof dish and top with lots of crumble (it tastes great when the crumble is thick!)

3. Bake for about 20 minutes. If the crumble begins to brown too quickly, cover it with foil for the remaining cooking time.

Peach, Ginger and Vanilla

Ingredients

8 peaches, peeled, stoned and chopped

1 tablespoon maple syrup

2 teaspoons ground cinnamon

2 teaspoons ground ginger

2 teaspoons vanilla extract

seeds from 1 vanilla pod

Method

1. Put all the ingredients into a saucepan with 2 tablespoons water and cook over a low heat for about 20 minutes, until the peaches have softened.

2. Spoon the mixture into the ramekins or pour it into the base of an ovenproof dish.

3. Cover with the crumble topping and bake for about 20 minutes. If the crumble begins to brown too quickly, cover it with foil for the remaining cooking time.

Banana and Almond Butter

Ingredients

4 bananas, sliced

4 tablespoons almond butter

4 tablespoons maple syrup

1 teaspoon ground cinnamon

1 teaspoon vanilla extract

Method

1. Put the almond butter, syrup, cinnamon and vanilla extract into a mixing bowl and stir thoroughly.

2. Line 8 ramekins with banana slices and pour over the mixture.

3. Pour the crumble topping over the filling and bake for about 20 minutes. If the crumble begins to brown too quickly, cover it with foil for the remaining cooking time.

4. Make this even more indulgent and serve with a scoop of Banana and Almond Butter Ice Cream (see page 220).

BASIL-INFUSED STRAWBERRIES *Serves 4*

I love this sweet strawberry treat with a big spoonful of coconut yogurt and a sprinkling of cinnamon. I think of this as my quintessentially British dessert.

Ingredients
375g strawberries, washed, hulled and halved or quartered
50g coconut or brown sugar, or to taste
juice of 2 lemons and zest of 1
a large handful of basil
freshly ground black pepper

Method
1. Put the strawberry pieces in a bowl and add the sugar, lemon zest and juice.

2. Pick the basil leaves and add them to the bowl. Add a crack of pepper and mix it all together.

3. Refrigerate until dessert time. The longer you leave it the more the strawberries will be infused with the basil – 1 hour is ideal.

CHOCOLATE CAKE WITH PEANUT BUTTER FROSTING *Makes 8–10*

This is mine and Chrissy's favourite dessert in the world and was our wedding cake! It's just so good for so many reasons and it will always bring back memories of the happiest moment of my life, ever.

Ingredients
75g raw cacao powder
270g plain flour
500g sugar
2 teaspoons baking soda
1 teaspoon sea salt
235ml vegetable oil
240ml sour cream
360ml water
2 teaspoons white wine vinegar
1 teaspoon vanilla extract
2 free-range eggs

For the frosting
125g soft butter
275g cream cheese
650g icing sugar
150g smooth peanut butter

Method
1. Preheat the oven to 180°C/gas mark 4. Line two 23cm round cake tins with baking parchment so you can effortlessly pull the cakes out when they're cooked.

2. Put the cocoa, flour, sugar, baking soda and salt into a food processor and cream together on a low speed. Next, add the oil and sour cream while continuing to beat on low. Slowly add the water, followed by the vinegar and vanilla extract and finally add the eggs.

3. Divide the cake mixture between the two tins and bake in the oven for 30–40 minutes. Leave to cool, then turn out onto a wire rack to cool completely.

4. To make the icing, beat the butter and cream cheese together until smooth. Gradually sift in the icing sugar, stirring to incorporate, then add the peanut butter and stir again.

5. Ice the cooled caked with the peanut butter frosting and serve.

BAKED APPLE WITH HONEY AND SPICED GREEK YOGURT *Serves 4*

This would also make a tasty breakfast if you are craving something sweet first thing, or if you're weaning yourself off sugary cereal.

Ingredients
4 Bramley apples
200ml Greek yogurt
1 tablespoon ground cinnamon
2 tablespoons honey (ideally Manuka)
1 teaspoon ground ginger
25g flaked almonds
2 tablespoons almond butter (optional)

Method
1 Preheat the oven to 180°C/gas mark 4. Line a baking tray with foil.
2. Push an apple corer into the centre of each apple, removing the seeds and stalks. If you don't have a corer use a small paring knife. Place on the prepared baking tray and bake for about 20 minutes, until the apples are cooked through.
3. Meanwhile, mix the Greek yogurt with the cinnamon, honey and ginger.
4. Spread the almonds on another baking tray and toast in the oven for a few minutes, until lightly golden.
5. Once the apples are cooked, slice them in half and serve with a big dollop of yogurt and a sprinkling of almonds. If you want to add to the indulgence, add a spoonful of almond butter on top of the yogurt.

COCONUT AND PISTACHIO BROWNIES *Makes 8–10*

Ingredients
65g butter
250g coconut palm sugar
1 free-range egg white
3 tablespoons raw cacao powder
125g self-raising gluten-free flour
a pinch of Himalayan pink salt
3 tablespoons coconut nectar blossom
3 tablespoons coconut oil, melted
50g pistachios, chopped

Method
1. Preheat the oven to 180°C/gas mark 4. Line a 20cm square cake tin or deep-sided baking tray with baking paper so you can pull the brownie out when it's cooked.
2. Put the butter and sugar into a food processor and cream it together on a low speed. Next add the egg white while continuing to beat on low. Slowly add the cacao powder and the flour.
3. Add the salt, coconut nectar blossom, coconut oil and the pistachios, and mix at a medium speed until just combined. Don't over mix it – it really just needs to be combined.
4. Pour the mixture into the lined tray and bake for 20 minutes.

NUT AND SEED FLAPJACKS *Makes 10–12*

These are a packed lunch treat for my daughter Charlotte (and for Chrissy and myself too!).

Ingredients
170g rolled oats
130g spelt flour
50g shredded coconut
50g raisins
25g chopped apricots
25g chopped prunes
20g pumpkin and sunflower seeds
100g coconut palm sugar
150g butter
2 tablespoons honey
1 tablespoon maple syrup
butter, for greasing

Method
1. Preheat the oven to 180°C/gas mark 4. Grease a baking tray with butter or line it with baking paper.

2. Mix all the dry ingredients together in a bowl.

3. Melt the butter, honey and syrup in a small pan over a low heat, or in the microwave.

4. Mix the wet ingredients into the dry ingredients, then tip into the prepared tray and press firmly.

5. Bake for 15–20 minutes, or until golden brown on top. Cool in the tin for a few minutes, then transfer to a wire rack to cool completely.

BUCKWHEAT CRÊPES WITH POACHED PLUMS AND HONEY *Makes 5–6*

Ingredients
4 eggs
130g buckwheat flour
2 teaspoons ground cinnamon
1 teaspoons vanilla extract
seeds from ½ vanilla pod
2 scoops Bodyism Body Brilliance
coconut oil, for frying
coconut yogurt, to serve
4 tablespoons maple syrup, to serve (optional)

For the poached plums
500g plums, washed, stoned and quartered
5 tablespoons maple syrup
1 teaspoon vanilla extract
1 teaspoon ground cinnamon
1 teaspoon ground ginger

Method
1. Put all the ingredients for the crêpes into a food-processor with 250ml water and blitz until the lumps have disappeared. Pour into a bowl and refrigerate for at least 30 minutes.

2. While the crêpe mixture is resting, place all the ingredients for the poached plums into a saucepan over a low heat with 225ml water and stir. Simmer for 15–20 minutes, until the plums have softened.

3. To cook the crêpes, melt the coconut oil in a non-stick frying pan over a low heat. Add a ladleful of the crêpe batter and rotate the pan so that it spreads evenly over the pan. Cook for a few minutes and once it lifts easily off the pan, flip it over and cook the other side for a few minutes, until golden brown.

4. Serve the crêpes with a spoonful of poached plums, some coconut yogurt and, if you want to be really indulgent, a drizzle of maple syrup.

BANANA AND ALMOND BUTTER ICE CREAM *Serves 8*

This is perfect for when you need to use up bananas and satisfy your sweet tooth at the same time! If you want to make this even more delicious add 4 scoops of Body Brilliance to boost your metabolism and give you a good dose of alkalizing supergreens.

Ingredients

4 bananas, chopped
250ml almond milk
3 tablespoons almond butter
1 teaspoon vanilla essence
1 teaspoon ground cinnamon
a pinch of salt

Method

1. Another seriously simple treat. Just put all the ingredients in a food processor and blitz. Pour in a tub and place in the freezer.
2. After a few hours stir the mixture well and put it back in the freezer to enjoy whenever you like.

BANANA, CHOCOLATE AND HAZELNUT ICE CREAM *Serves 8*

Ingredients

85g roasted hazelnuts
4 bananas
2 dates, pitted
250ml almond milk
2 tablespoons raw cacao powder
1 teaspoon vanilla essence
a pinch of salt

Method

1. Blitz the hazelnuts in a food processor until you have a nut butter. Spoon the butter into a mixing bowl with the rest of the ingredients. Mix well.
2. Pour the mixture back into the food processor and blitz again.
3. Pour into a tub and freeze for a few hours, stir, then put back in the freezer until you seek a sweet treat.

COCONUT, AVOCADO AND CACAO NIB ICE POPS *Serves 2*

Ingredients
1 large ripe avocado
250ml coconut milk
4 tablespoons maple syrup or raw honey
a squeeze of lemon juice
50g cacao nibs

Method
1. Place all the ingredients except the cacao nibs into a blender and blitz on high until smooth.

2. Mix in the cacao nibs and divide the mixture between ice-pop moulds. Freeze for at least 6 hours before eating.

AMOR (PEAR) POLENTA CAKE *Serves 6–8*

Ingredients
4 pears, quartered and poached (see page 210)
85g coconut oil, melted
200g xylitol
2 teaspoons vanilla extract
2 teaspoons almond extract
a pinch of sea salt
2 teaspoons ground cinnamon
4 eggs
100g ground almonds
340g polenta
2 teaspoons baking powder

Method
1. Preheat the oven to 180°C/gas mark 4. Grease and line a 20cm round cake tin.

2. Poach the pears using the recipe on page 210, reserving the syrup to drizzle over the cake.

3. Whisk the coconut oil, xylitol, vanilla extract, almond extract, salt and cinnamon together until light and fluffy. Beat in the eggs one by one, then stir in the ground almonds, polenta and baking powder. Mix until well combined.

4. Pour the batter into the cake tin and arrange the poached pear slices on top, pushing them into the top of the cake mix slightly.

5. Cook for 30 minutes until cooked all the way through (test by inserting a skewer and check it comes out clean). If the cake turns golden brown before it is fully cooked, cover with foil and continue to bake.

6. Once cooked, remove the cake from the oven and leave to cool. Using a skewer, prick the surface of the cake all over with tiny holes and then pour the poached pear juice over the cake so that the liquid seeps in (it helps make it perfectly moist).

7. Serve with a spoon of Banana and Almond Butter Ice Cream (see page 220)!

Top tip!
A great alternative to
shop-bought sugar-filled
ice lollies. The avocado
gives the pop a deliciously
creamy texture and the
nibbs add the perfect
crunch.

GINGER CACAO BALLS *Makes 10–12*

Ingredients
175g dates, pitted
140g raw cashews
1 tablespoon raw cacao powder
1 tablespoon ground ginger
½ teaspoon vanilla extract
a pinch of Himalayan pink salt
a handful of coconut flakes

Method
1. Put all the ingredients except the coconut into a food processor and blitz until combined.
2. Roll tablespoons of the mixture between the palms of your hands to make balls.
3. Tip the coconut flakes onto a shallow plate and roll the cacao balls in them to coat. Refrigerate until ready to eat.

BLISS BALLS *Makes 10 balls*

These balls are the perfect guilt-free sweet treat, or pre- or post-gym snack. The flavour variations are endless. Store them in the freezer and then you can just grab and go.

Ingredients
For the basic mix
12 dates, pitted
50g blanched hazelnuts
1 tablespoon almond butter
1 tablespoon cacao nibs

Method
1. Blitz all the ingredients in a food processor.
2. If you want to stick with the basic mix (which is still seriously tasty), simply roll into balls between the palms of your hands and store in an airtight container in the freezer. Alternatively, add the ingredients as listed below before shaping.

Chocolate Orange Bliss

Ingredients
1 x quantity Bliss Ball basic mix
1 tablespoon raw cacao powder
1 teaspoon orange extract

Bounty Bliss

Ingredients
1 x quantity Bliss Ball basic mix
1 tablespoon raw cacao powder
1 teaspoon coconut oil
2 tablespoons desiccated coconut

Mocha Melts

Ingredients
1 x quantity Bliss Ball basic mix
1 tablespoon raw cacao powder
1 shot of espresso

Gingerbread Bliss

Ingredients
1 x quantity Bliss Ball basic mix
1 teaspoon ground ginger
1 teaspoon ground cinnamon
1 teaspoon maple syrup

Goji and Chocolate

Ingredients
1 x quantity Bliss Ball basic mix
1 tablespoon raw cacao powder
1 tablespoon goji berries
1 teaspoon coconut oil

Snicker Glory

Ingredients
1 x quantity Bliss Ball basic mix
1 tablespoon almond butter
1 tablespoon raw cacao powder
1 tablespoon maple syrup
1 tablespoon quinoa pops
1 teaspoon coconut oil
1 teaspoon vanilla extract

CASHEW AND CAROB COOKIES *Makes 15–20*

These naturally gluten-free cookies should come with a warning sign – they are seriously addictive!
They will last for weeks in a cookie tin (although I doubt it'll be more than a few days).

Ingredients
200g cashew butter
100g softened unsalted butter
75g coconut palm sugar
1 teaspoon bicarbonate of soda
a pinch of Himalayan pink salt
1 teaspoon vanilla extract
1 teaspoon carob syrup
1 large egg, lightly beaten
175g ground almonds
1 teaspoon carob powder
50g cashews, chopped
25g cacao nibs (optional)

Method
1. Preheat the oven to 180°C/gas mark 4. Line 2 baking trays with baking paper.

2. Put the cashew butter and softened butter into a food processor and mix on low for 1 minute. Add the sugar and mix for a further 2 minutes until creamed. Still on a low speed, add the bicarbonate of soda, salt, vanilla, carob syrup and egg.

3. Fold in the ground almonds with a metal spoon, making sure you don't overmix. Fold in the carob powder, cashews and cacao nibs, if using.

4. Shape spoonfuls of mixture between the palms of your hands into 5cm balls and place on the baking trays, about 5cm apart. Flatten each one ever so lightly with a fork, sprinkle with a teeny bit more pink salt and bake for 10–12 minutes, keeping an eye on them as they can easily overcook. Once they start to brown around the edges they are done.

5. Remove from the oven and leave to cool on the tray for 5 minutes before transferring to a wire rack to cool completely.

ROSEMARY AND LEMON OAT BISCUITS *Makes 15–20*

Ingredients
210g plain flour, sifted
1 teaspoon ground cinnamon
140g rolled oats
50g caster sugar
zest of 1 lemon
1 long sprig rosemary, leaves
removed and finely chopped
75g shredded coconut
1 tablespoon golden syrup
or treacle
1 tablespoon honey
150g chopped unsalted butter
½ teaspoon bicarbonate of soda
1½ tablespoons water
Himalayan pink salt

Method
1. Preheat oven to 180°C/gas mark 4. Line 2 baking trays with baking paper.

2. Place the flour, cinnamon, oats, sugar, lemon zest, rosemary and coconut in a large bowl and stir to combine.

3. Put the golden syrup, honey and butter into a small saucepan over a low heat and stir until the butter is melted. Remove from heat and stir in the bicarbonate of soda along with 1½ tablespoons water.

4. Pour the wet ingredients into the dry ingredients and mix together until fully combined.

5. Roll spoonfuls of mixture between the palms of your hands to make balls and place them on the lined baking trays, pressing down on the tops to flatten them slightly. Bake for 12 minutes or until golden brown.

6. As soon as you remove them from the oven, sprinkle the biscuits with a little of the Himalayan pink salt.

ORANGE, GRAPEFRUIT AND TURMERIC CAKE *Serves 8*

Ingredients
For the cake
1 orange

1 grapefruit

3 free-range eggs

75g coconut palm sugar

200g ground almonds

65g soy or tapioca flour

1cm piece fresh turmeric, grated

1 teaspoon baking powder

For the syrup (optional)
rind and juice of 1 orange

50g coconut palm sugar

Method
1. Preheat the oven to 180°C/gas mark 4. Grease a 20cm springform cake tin and line it with baking paper.

2. Put the orange and grapefruit in a saucepan, cover with cold water, bring to the boil and cook for 15 minutes. Drain and repeat. Coarsely chop both skin and flesh and remove the seeds. Transfer to a blender with a splash of cold water and pulse until smooth.

3. Beat the eggs and sugar in a mixing bowl until thick and pale. Add the orange and grapefruit mixture, ground almonds, soy or tapioca flour, turmeric and baking powder and fold to combine. Pour the mixture into the prepared cake tin and bake for 1 hour, or until a skewer inserted into the centre comes out clean. Set aside for about 15 minutes to cool while you make the syrup, if using.

4. To make the syrup, boil the orange rind for 5 minutes in a little water to soften it, then drain and return to the pan. Add the juice and sugar and heat on low, stirring constantly, for about 3 minutes, or until the sugar dissolves and the mixture becomes syrupy.

5. Gently poke holes all over the top of the cake with a skewer and spoon the syrup over it. Serve warm or at room temperature.

CHILLI CHOCOLATE TART *Serves 8–10*

Chrissy and I are big chocolate fans so when we choose to have a naughty treat, this is one of our top picks. If you are gluten intolerant, swap the flour for a gluten-free equivalent.

Ingredients
For the pastry
150g butter, softened
25g coconut palm sugar, packed firm
50g raw cacao powder
2 teaspoons honey
250g plain flour
a pinch of salt

For the filling
2 medium or hot chillies, chopped
600g double cream
400g dark chocolate, 70% cocoa solids, broken into small pieces

Method
1. Preheat the oven to 200°C/gas mark 6. Lightly grease a 30cm tart tin.

2. Cream the butter and sugar in a bowl until light, fluffy and white, then add the cacao and honey and continue to beat for 1 minute. Add the flour and a pinch of salt and stir to combine. Wrap the dough in baking paper and chill in the fridge for about 1 hour, or in the freezer for 20 minutes.

3. To make the filling, poach the chillies in the cream over a low heat for about 20 minutes. Taste as you go to stop it getting too hot for your palate. Scoop out the chillies, squeeze out all the cream and discard the chillies.

4. Add the chocolate to the warm chilli cream and gently whisk until it dissolves and you have a glossy, smooth ganache. Cool in the fridge.

5. Take the dough from the fridge and roll it out so that it's just bigger than your tart tin. Use it to line the tin, prick the bottom lightly with a fork and blind bake for about 20 minutes until lightly golden. Remove from the oven and leave to cool.

6. Pour the ganache into the cooled tart case and put in the fridge to chill and set for at least 1 hour before serving.

CHOCOLATE QUINOA COOKIES *Makes 10*

If anyone says you have to compromise on taste if you want to eat cleanly, bake them a batch of these cookies and they will very quickly be eating their words. These are my go-to treats and once you've tried them you'll know why.

Ingredients
70g coconut oil, melted
75g coconut palm sugar
1 teaspoon vanilla extract
1 egg
65g quinoa flour (to make, blitz quinoa flakes in a food processor)
60g gluten-free oats
½ teaspoon bicarbonate of soda
¼ teaspoon Himalayan pink salt
2 scoops Bodyism Body Brilliance (optional)
50g cacao nibs

Method
1. Preheat the oven to 180°C/gas mark 4. Line 2 baking trays with baking paper.

2. Put the melted coconut oil and coconut palm sugar into a bowl and mix together. Add the vanilla extract and egg and stir well.

3. In a separate bowl, mix together the quinoa flour, oats, bicarbonate of soda, salt and Body Brilliance, if using.

4. Stir the liquid mixture into the quinoa mixture, add the cacao nibs and stir well.

5. Roll a spoonful of mixture into a ball and then flatten it onto the lined baking tray. Continue until you have used up all the mixture, leaving 5cm between each cookie as they will spread in the oven.

6. Bake for 8–10 minutes (depending how crispy or gooey you like them), remove the tray from the oven and set aside to cool and firm up on the tray.

Your Desserts
BAD, BETTER & BEST TABLES

BAD	BETTER	BEST
Chocolate Ice Cream High in fat and not the good kind! Most shop bought ice creams are also packed with preservatives, sugar and artificial products.	**Chocolate Coconut Ice Cream** Dairy-free options can sit better with our digestion, however they often still contain hidden sugar and preservatives.	**Banana, Chocolate and Hazelnut Ice Cream (page 220)** Ditch the heavy cream and processed versions and enjoy something just as tasty without any of the nasties.
Shop-bought frozen apple crumble High in sugar, flour and with little nutritional value	**Homemade apple crumble and ice cream** You can choose the ingredients that are going into it and so avoid preservatives. If possible, choose organic fruit.	**A Trio of Crumbles (page 212) with coconut yogurt** The crumble topping is packed with superfoods and the coconut yogurt is a perfect dairy-free addition.
Eton mess Full of sugar and fat and very little nutrient content.	**Strawberries and cream** The fruit contains wonderful nutrients, but non-organic strawberries can be heavily sprayed with pesticides.	**Organic strawberries with organic cream and flaked almonds** Full of antioxidants and good fats. The almonds will also give a great source of protein.
Pancakes with jam Loaded with sugar and the refined flour will leave your tummy unhappy.	**Gluten-free pancakes with maple syrup** These pancakes will at least contain less irritants, but they still may be high in sugar. Maple syrup is a natural sweetener that has more nutritious qualities.	**Buckwheat Crêpes with Poached Plums and Honey (page 218)** Buckwheat is a powerhouse of a grain and is naturally gluten free. Raw honey is a wonderful natural sweetener.
Shop-bought chocolate mousse This really is a sugar bomb. I wish there were some health benefits but there are none at all.	**Homemade chocolate mousse using over 70% dark solids** High-quality chocolate has less sugar than the cheaper version.	**Chocolate, Orange and Avocado Mousse (page 210)** The avocado gives a great source of healthy fats and makes it more filling, which means you will feel satisfied for longer.

Clean and Lean desserts and treats will not only satisfy your sweet tooth but also have some wonderful health benefits. However, don't fool yourself into thinking that you can indulge in 'healthy' treats every day. Even though they're nutritious and unprocessed there is still often a high amount of sugar in there and too much sugar will leave you tired, lethargic and moody and possibly overweight.

BAD	BETTER	BEST
Tinned fruit cocktail Tinned fruit contains a huge amount of sugars. The fruit loses its nutrient content too.	**Shop-bought fruit salad** Obviously fresher than a tinned version but often the quality of the fruit is still very low.	**Homemade fruit salad** Add lots of berries as these contain less sugar than most fruits and are packed with antioxidants.
Brie, crackers and chutney Chutneys are laden with sugar and brie is really high in fat.	**Grass-fed cheese and spelt crackers** Grass-fed cheese is much less processed and therefore has a better nutrient value. Spelt contains less gluten than the refined version so it is a kinder flour for your digestive system.	**Organic Parmesan with flaxseed crackers** Parmesan has a lower lactose level than other cheeses which is great for those that often suffer after drinking milk. Flaxseed is a fantastic source of fibre.
Shop-bought slice of chocolate cake Sorry, but this is just a sugar bomb and is generally made with low-quality ingredients.	**Flourless chocolate cake** The lack of gluten means it contains less irritants but it will still be packed with sugar.	**Bliss Balls (page 224)** The chocolate variety of these delicious balls gives you the delicious cocoa flavours but without any of the processed add ons.
Jelly Full of sugar and artificial flavourings.	**Jelly with fruit** The add on of fruit will offer some nutrients.	**Basil-infused strawberries (page 215)** These are perfectly sweet but without the bad stuff. Basil is thought to be a great stress buster too.

chapter 9

Drinks
and
Smoothies

MORNING METABOLIC MOCHA *Serves 1*

Sometimes we all need an extra kick to wake us up in the morning. This seriously easy smoothie does just that while providing you with a healthy dose of protein.

Ingredients
1 banana
1 scoop Bodyism Body Brilliance
125ml almond milk
115ml coconut water
1 tablespoon raw cacao powder
1 teaspoon ground coffee
¼ red chilli, chopped (optional)

Method
1. Add all the ingredients to the blender and blitz. (If you want an even stronger kick, add ¼ chopped red chilli into the mix!)

PURIFICATION TONIC *Serves 2*

If you are feeling under the weather and really need to seriously boost your system then this tonic is for you. This is a fiery concoction that is a character building experience but will leave you feeling stronger for it.

Ingredients
3 garlic cloves, peeled
1cm piece fresh ginger, peeled
2.5cm piece fresh turmeric, peeled
zest of 1 lemon
300ml apple cider vinegar
2 tablespoons raw honey
a pinch of cayenne pepper

Method
1. Put the garlic, ginger, turmeric and lemon zest into an extraction juicer. (If you don't have a juicer, grate the roots and garlic and squeeze out the juice.)
2. Add all the other ingredients, stir and drink.

Top tip!
A smoothie can be a great snack or, depending on the ingredients, even a great meal when you're on the go.

CLEANER COLADA *Serves 1*

This is a delicious treat that should be enjoyed instead of a sugar-filled chemical cocktail, otherwise known as a milkshake (unless you make it yourself). This will satisfy the cravings of even the most desperate sugar addict while also giving you the health benefits that your body needs. Why pineapple? It may be high in sugar but it also has the benefit of some really wonderful digestive enzymes.

Ingredients
½ banana, chopped
½ avocado, chopped
250ml coconut water
60g pineapple, sliced and chopped
2 tablespoons coconut yogurt
a handful of spinach
3 ice cubes

Method
1. Simply put all the ingredients into a blender and blitz.

GRAPEFRUIT, CARROT AND TURMERIC SMOOTHIE *Serves 1*

This is a great anti-inflammatory detoxing smoothie.

Ingredients
3 carrots, chopped
1 pink grapefruit, peeled and segmented
250ml filtered water
2.5cm piece of fresh turmeric, peeled
0.5cm piece of fresh ginger, peeled
a pinch of Himalayan pink sea salt

Method
1. Simply put all the ingredients into a blender and blitz.

Top tip!
A smoothie in the morning can create the foundation for a happy healthy day, or it can provide a nourishing health boost to keep you going.

BURN BERRY BURN *Serves 1*

Ingredients
1 scoop Bodyism Berry Burn
250ml coconut water
a handful of frozen berries

Method
1. Put all the ingredients into a blender and blitz to your preferred consistency.

ROSEMARY SMOOTHIE *Serves 1*

Ingredients
1 banana
250ml filtered water
100g blueberries
50g baby spinach
1 tablespoon chia seeds
1 tablespoon coconut oil
1 rosemary sprig, leaves removed
and finely chopped

Method
1. Put all the ingredients into a blender and blitz to your preferred consistency.

***Top tip!**
Rosemary is a mood
booster – sprinkle it
on anything when you're
feeling low and want a
DIY stress buster.*

EGGNOG *Serves 6–8*

This is a cheat meal when Christmas comes and you want to get all fancy in the kitchen. The benefit here is that you are getting the protein from the eggs but let's be honest, this is definitely a treat.

Ingredients

6 eggs, chilled
100g coconut palm sugar
½ teaspoon vanilla extract
1 tablespoon maple syrup
¼ teaspoon grated nutmeg, plus extra for dusting
¼ teaspoon ground cardamom
¼ teaspoon of ground cinnamon
100ml full-fat milk, chilled
200ml double cream, chilled
crushed ice

Method

1. Beat the eggs until frothy. Beat in the sugar, vanilla, maple syrup and spices.
2. Slowly stir in the milk, then the cream.
3. Strain and serve over crushed ice with a dusting of grated nutmeg.

BRILLIANCE CHOCOLATE MOUSSE *Serves 2*

Bodyism Body Brilliance is a nutritious body friendly treat full of nourishing supergreens and metabolism-boosting green tea extracts. This is great pre- or post-workout or anytime you feel like you need to give your body a hug from the inside out. It's a little thick to drink with a straw so enjoy with a spoon!

Ingredients

1 ripe avocado, peeled and stoned
1 tablespoon raw cacao powder
2 scoops Bodyism Body Brilliance
2 tablespoons maple syrup
¼ teaspoon ground ginger (optional)
30g fresh or frozen berries

Method

1. Blend the avocado flesh, cacao, Body Brilliance, maple syrup and ginger until smooth.
2. Stir through the berries and divide into airtight containers. Refrigerate for 2 hours or overnight.
3. Throw in your bag for the perfect mid-morning energy booster.

BRILLIANT CHOCOLATE ALMOND MILK *Serves 3*

Ingredients

140g raw almonds, soaked overnight in 750ml water

2 dates, pitted (optional – this may be too sweet)

3 scoops Bodyism Body Brilliance

1 tablespoon raw cacao powder

1 teaspoon ground cinnamon

1 teaspoon vanilla extract

Method

1. Rinse the soaked almonds and put them in a blender with 500ml water.

2. Place a nut milk bag or a muslin cloth over a mixing bowl and slowly pour the nut milk into the bowl. You will need to gently squeeze the mixture to extract all the milk. Discard the pulp.

3. Pour the almond milk into a blender with the remaining ingredients. Blitz well and serve over ice.

Top tip!
Almonds are notoriously difficult to milk (especially wild almonds that are known to bite and scratch); so the alternative is to soak them in a bowl first.

HAIR, SKIN AND NAIL ELIXIR *Serves 2*

If you can't find our supplements, find a good-quality alternative. Please remember, you get what you pay for; try to find good-quality natural protein sources.

Ingredients
500ml almond milk
120g frozen berries
1 scoop Bodyism Beauty Food
1 scoop Bodyism Protein
Excellence Vanilla

Method
1. Blend all the ingredients and serve immediately.

SWEET-POTATO PIE SMOOTHIE *Serves 2*

Ingredients
500ml almond milk
65g roasted sweet potato
1 scoop Bodyism Protein
Excellence Vanilla
½ teaspoon ground cinnamon
½ teaspoon ground ginger
¼ teaspoon vanilla powder
(optional)
handful of ice (optional)

Method
1. Seriously simple, just blitz up all the ingredients until smooth.

Top tip!
This is a great low-GI source of carbs and it tastes delicious too.

1

Your 7-day
BEAUTY MENU PLANNER

	BREAKFAST	SNACK
monday	The Cup of Life Page 75	Tegan's Beauty Bites Page 199
tuesday	Apple, Pear and Rosemary Pancakes Page 77	Cinnamon Spiced Nuts Page 202
wednesday	Turmeric and Spinach Scramble Page 87	Quinoa and Carob balls Page 180
thursday	Spinach and Avocado Egg Wrap Page 83	Rosemary Cacao Balls Page 199
friday	Egg and Avocado Bake Page 81	Cayenne and Wasabi Baked Chickeas Page 181
saturday	Protein Pancakes Page 71	Apple Crisps with Almond Butter Page 200
sunday	Shakshuka Page 88	Nori wraps Page 180

This is a wonderfully nourishing menu plan packed full of antioxidants with the health of your hair, skin and nails in mind with every meal.

LUNCH	SMOOTHIES	DINNER
Soup of Eternal Youth served with some grilled salmon Page 100	Hair, Skin and Nail Elixir Page 247	Asian Salmon Bites with Avocado Dip Page 148
Tuna, Bean and Herb Salad Page 124	Grapefruit, Carrot and Turmeric Smoothie Page 238	Herby Poached Fish served with steamed greens Page 151
Healing Bone Broth Page 100	Burn Berry Burn Page 241	Lamb Summer Stew served with steamed greens Page 167
Asian Chicken Wraps Page 121	Rosemary Smoothie Page 241	Kale-stuffed Baked Trout Page 147
Tomato and Bean Salad with Lemon-grilled Mackerel Page 127	Cleaner Colada Page 238	Sexy Pesto on salmon with fresh greens Page 134
Beetroot and Wild Fennel Soup served with a Clean and Lean protein if you feel you need it Page 94	Hair, Skin and Nail Elixir Page 247	Chickpea-stuffed Turkey Roast Page 162
Asian Red Cabbage Salad with Glazed Salmon Page 125	Grapefruit, Carrot and Turmeric Smoothie Page 238	Chicken and Leek Quinoa Risotto Page 138

Your 7-day
ENERGY MENU PLANNER

	BREAKFAST	SNACK
monday	Cacao, Carob and Coconut Granola Page 64	Cinnamon Spiced Nuts Page 202
tuesday	Coconut and Cacao Clusters Page 67	Seed Crackers Page 179
wednesday	Spinach and Avocado Egg Wrap Page 83	Courgette and Carrot Crackers Page 181
thursday	Cinnamon and Baked Apple Oatmeal Page 68	Nori Wraps Page 180
friday	Egg, Chia and Rainbow Chard Muffins Page 72	Clean and Lean Bread Page 197
saturday	Apple, Pear and Rosemary Pancakes Page 77	Tegan's Banana Protein Balls Page 199
sunday	Super Porridge Page 70	Parsnip and Celeriac Fries Page 176

This is a life affirming, energising collection of delicious meals, designed to help you achieve a healthy, vibrant and happy body.

LUNCH	SMOOTHIES	DINNER
Avocado, Bean and Mango Salsa with Spiced Prawns Page 119	Burn Berry Burn Page 241	Coconut Lentil Curry Page 142
Asian Chicken Wraps Page 121	Brilliant Chocolate Almond Milk Page 245	Sweet Potato Fish Pie Page 152
Butternut Squash and Chestnut Soup Page 97	Burn Berry Burn Page 241	Sweet and Sour Chicken Page 157
Easy Peasy Chickpea Pizza Page 107	Cleaner Colada Page 238	Shepherd's Pie Page 166
Ricotta Pies with Courgette Carpaccio Page 116	Eggnog Page 244	Chickpea-stuffed Turkey Roast Page 162
Buckwheat Crêpes with Ratatouille Page 112	Morning Metabolic Mocha Page 236	Chicken Nuggets and Sweet Potato Fries Page 161
Sea Bass with Beetroot and Fennel Slaw Page 120	Brilliant Chocolate Almond Milk Page 245	Green Gnocchi Page 132

3 Your 7-day
WEIGHT LOSS MENU PLANNER

	BREAKFAST	SNACK
monday	Green Goodness Page 64	Cayenne and Wasabi Baked Chickpeas Page 181
tuesday	Lemon and Coconut Chia Pudding Page 72	Carrot, Beet and Kale Crisps Page 176
wednesday	Yogurt Page 68	Tegan's Beauty Bites Page 199
thursday	Spinach and Avocado Egg Wrap Page 83	Cinnamon Spiced Nuts Page 202
friday	Turmeric and Spinach Scramble Page 87	Tegan's Chocolate Serenity Balls Page 199
saturday	Egg and Avocado Bake Page 81	Apple Crisps with Almond Butter Page 200
sunday	Avocado and Turkey Ham Fingers Page 84	Seed Crackers Page 179

Your 7-day weight loss menu planner is a reminder that the fastest way to lose weight is to focus on your health and the best way to get a permanent fix is to focus on the long term.

LUNCH	SMOOTHIES	DINNER
Shredded Kale and Mushroom Asian salad Page 108	Burn Berry Burn Page 241	Courgetti with Kale Pesto Page 135
Chopped Salad Page 115	Purification Tonic Page 236	Bejewelled Aubergine Page 136
Sea Bass with Beetroot and Fennel Slaw Page 120	Grapefruit, Carrot and Turmeric Smoothie Page 238	Herby Poached Fish Page 151
Soup of Eternal Youth Page 100	Rosemary Smoothie Page 241	Turmeric Turkey Burgers with Pickled Courgettes Page 160
Beetroot and Wild Fennel Soup Page 94	Burn Berry Burn Page 241	Middle Eastern-Style Trout with Cauliflower Rice Page 143
Courgette, Feta and Griddled Peach Salad Page 124	Grapefruit, Carrot and Turmeric Smoothie Page 238	Green Gnocchi Page 132
Quinoa Tabbouleh Page 104	Metabolic Mocha Page 236	James' Mum's Chicken Curry Page 142

acknowledgements

There are always so many people to thank. Far too many to fit on a page. Chrissy and myself are just so incredibly grateful to all the people who have helped us create this wonderful message. Firstly our friend and partner, Ferit – thank you from the bottom of our hearts for believing in us. You have made the impossible, possible for us. To Luke, Chantal, Jake and Sienna, thank you for being the truest of friends. To Sol for showing us that fortune truly does favour the brave. To Maria for helping us write this beautiful book and to Rebecca for writing lovely recipes. To Daniella for your passion and brilliance and for never taking no for an answer – you're a super star. To Tevfik for your unwavering support. To Nathalie for more than words could ever do justice. To Emilia for having a heart of gold.

And finally to my father. You taught me that being gentle and strong go hand in hand. I would give everything I have just for one more day with you... So thank you for teaching me to cherish every moment I have with the people I love.

This is my dad, comforting me just before he passed away.
He carried me every day.